Triple Death: Embers of Terror

Robert Algeri

PO Box 221974 Anchorage, Alaska 99522-1974
books@publicationconsultants.com—www.publicationconsultants.com

ISBN Number: 978-1-59433-949-3
eBook ISBN Number: 978-1-59433-950-9

Library of Congress Number: 2020951619

—First Edition—

Manufactured in the United States of America

Disclaimer

This is a work of fiction based on actual events.

Any resemblance to actual persons, living or dead, is purely coincidental and unintentional. The people and places are products of the author's imagination.
Events surrounding the case of prolific serial killer Robert Hansen provide the backdrop for this story.
None of the stories in this book should be construed as having been a factual part of those events.
Dedicated to the victims who fell. May God rest their souls.
Approved by author Robert Algeri, aka Romeo Foxtrot.

Heartfelt thanks to my wife Diane,
Evan Swensen of Publication
Consultants, and all my supporters and readers.

Contents

Introduction

Prolific Alaskan Serial Killer Robert Hansen

Robert Hansen surmised that he had regaled us with his eminence.

We observe him writhing to a silent beat within his head and dancing ritualistically naked around the fire with nothing but his boots and glasses on.

White-hot embers flaring, he starts howling into the moonless night like a victorious wolf; he stomps.

Growling and slinking into the confines of his hidden lair, he begins to pound heavily upon his chest.

Alaskan serial killer Robert Hansen. Master of nefarious crime? Copycat serial killer? Pretender to the throne?

Opening Interlude

The Maestro: Anchorage Street Savage

Like a great white shark prowling beneath the deep, you don't ever want him to think you are trying to take something away from him. He will eviscerate you, tear you in two, and toss your cold limp body into Cook Inlet just for fun.

How's he getting away with all this? How is it that the people who supposedly know in this town don't know? Is Maestro a CID officer? Is Maestro a CIA agent? How do you get away with running an international human trafficking ring with this group of miscreants? In a city like Anchorage, Alaska?

Supplying transnational elite with dream makers and dream fulfillers. The minimum buy-in is US$1 million. This buys you the privilege of hunting another human being in a pre-prepared graveyard adorned with artifacts of the occult.

For US$2 million, you can handpick your victim, engage in a sexual fantasy with them for 24–48 hours, and then fly out from the sex den in a small airplane with them: victims chained in cages, wide eyed and disheveled, tossed into the cabin like cargo, their basic needs unattended.

First Glimpse
The Stiletto: Alaskan Street Tough

Anchorage, Alaska, 1981.
I find myself sauntering along dust-strewn Fourth Avenue in downtown Anchorage, Alaska, with my roommate Keith from Fort Richardson.

We are about to enter the Wild Cherry; it is a notoriously dark and shadowy confine filled with stale smoke and broken dreams. *I have no idea what to expect, because*

I have never been inside of an exotic dance club before. Why am I even doing this?

As we enter the dingy confine, slow-moving shadows silhouetted against a green spotlight begin to emerge as writhing flesh, hot and steamy, bouncing to the beat. We take a seat over near the front door at a small round table that has been branded with burn marks from many careless unattended cigarettes over the countless years.

Seated next to us at another small table is a solitary man. Keith kicks me under the table and quickly nods his head toward the lone brooding man who is sitting next to us. Keith leans his head close in toward me. "Look at this freak. It's fifty-eight degrees outside, and he is sitting in a strip club wearing wool hunting clothes. Including his hat. Look at this guy; look at him."

I attempt to turn my head in a casually calm and relaxed manner, when my eyes fall on a man who is dressed in full hunting clothes from his head down to his feet.

It is a commonly seen hunting pattern of small buffalo check that is sold in two basic color combinations. He is wearing a green-and-black combination. His thick wool hat is made of the same buffalo check pattern. He has the ear flaps pulled back, exposing the puffy white liner inside.

His jacket looks brand new. It is shiny green and black, waiting to be exposed to the abusive elements of Alaska while offering to protect its wearer from untold dire consequences. His pants are all black, and they also look like wool. His feet are entombed in heavy hunting boots that come up to the middle of his calves.

He is looking down at the table with both of his hands wrapped around a glass that he seems to be peering aimlessly into. He looks up at Keith and me while nodding his head once upward. With his left hand, he reaches up and deftly pushes on the bridge of his glasses. Nervously his eyes dart back down into his empty, gloomy glass.

A harried waitress comes over, and she starts speaking to us, "Are you guys drinking today?"

Keith blurts out, "Yes, ma'am. Would you please grab us two beers from the tap? Anything cold will do it for us."

Loudly she replies, "Everyone saw you two looking at this creep over here; he always comes in here and never buys a dance. He just watches while the girls dance for other people. We want to keep him out of here, but the owner has asked us to back off him."

She glares over toward the man, but he never acknowledges what is being said about him. He just keeps looking down into his empty glass.

Keith motions into the crowd for a dancer—a beautiful, bubbly blonde girl comes quickly running over and introduces herself. "Hi, I'm Sherry. What will we be doing for you guys today?"

Keith replies, "Sherry, I want a table dance, and I want you to dance for us, My name is Keith, and this is my roommate Tony. We are from Fort Richardson."

Sherry replies, "Keith, Tony, it is very nice to meet you two. Please let me sit with you guys until the next song starts."

When our waitress returns with our beer, she leans over and shouts into Sherry's ear, "Let's see if Resident Weirdo over here is going to start his peeping act or not."

Her hands go to her hips. With toes tapping, she starts shooting stern looks his way.

As the next song begins to play, Sherry stands up and starts bouncing with the beat, and sure enough, Resident Weirdo steals a glance her way. We make sure he can see us scowling at him, and he quickly looks back down at his hands.

Sherry moves into a position that he can't seem to resist, so he leans back and turns his head while staring at her with his laser-like glare.

Keith snaps. He jumps up and screams, "That's it. You're out of here, man." With a menacing growl, he grabs the lonely hunter, and all of the girls start screaming, "Get him out of here. We don't want him in here anymore."

A melee occurs, and I find myself scuffling with Keith and the weird man inside the entrance of the Wild Cherry. Finally we get him pushed out onto the sidewalk.

Keith is yelling at him, "Don't come back in here. Now scram, come on. Get lost now."

The man is awkwardly standing there out on the sidewalk of E Fourth Avenue. He keeps looking down at the cracked sidewalk while shuffling his feet.

When he looks back up at us, his left hand deftly pushes on the bridge of his glasses. He turns around and silently slinks back across the empty street from whence he must have come.

Second Glimpse
Damon Dirks: Alaskan Serial Killer

Anchorage, Alaska, 1981.

Lately, I've been feeling a little adrift. Chechakos, I am no Chechakos, my friends.

Over the hill and around the bend, into the sunset together for one last dance we shall go.

Bondage, her restraints reflect my roaring flames. She becomes a savage, raw with heavy tears. Her emotions are epic as the realization sets in. Jade will not be going home tonight because she is about to become dead.

Let me build my fire up into a blazing inferno. Let its flames threaten to ignite the surrounding forest while I dance mockingly around her and the pre-dug grave I have prepared for her. I have studied her for months. I have been watching her every move, flittering like a lost dove lightly across a dimly lit stage. *Is she eager for my finale? Is she enjoying the show?*

She once stood before the people shimmering like a queen; now I have stripped her down.

Beaten and bruised, Jade watches as I mirror her every move, I am sadistic and full of eager pleasure with my dance, and my hips are gyrating to the long-lost beat within my head.

Writhing, ritualistically dancing naked around the fire with nothing but my boots and glasses on, I've become a depraved, chillingly mocking, and sadistic predator. I have the stench of a victorious wolf howling; now I stand growling long into the moonless night.

The final shudder of her dying body pulsing through my stiff, claw-like fingers becomes my lasting reward. It becomes engraved into every fiber of my muscles and body.

A gentle breeze rings the wind chimes hanging in the tree above my head. Jade's left foot is still quivering, scraping at the dried leaves. I press my foot down on her ankle to stop the movement and silence her last attempt at escape.

She was a fighter. Her fingers of fury slashed across my trachea and drew blood; now I will need to explain the injury to my wife.

I need to do one last thing before I leave my little baby to her sleep. I have an extremely beautiful and delicate dream catcher to hang above her grave. I like to make sure all my ladies are kept in good company during my absence.

I have become a cunning predator and extremely manipulative. I've learned to slink within the shadows. I did not come to Alaska to give. I came to take from the bounty of the land.

Third Glimpse
The Maestro: Alaskan Dealer of Flesh

Anchorage, Alaska, 1981.

I didn't move to Alaska to be pushed around by anybody. I am going to take what I want when I want it. I will not be made a monkey of in this man's town. Do I look like your monkey? Am I your monkey?

I have a piece of every business from Anchorage down to the Homer Spit. I have a piece of the liquor industry, after-hours night clubs, video stores, adult entertainment facilities, and Orange taxi-cab company. I have created more jobs in Anchorage, Alaska, than any politician or single company has in the last twenty-five years of this state's history, and you can quote me on that.

I was able to secure and organize the Homer docks and take control of all the incoming drug activity flowing in on the fishing boats. Fishermen often soften with money—like most people they are very easily bought when times seem tough.

This is how you know the true value of a man—can he be bought? When it comes to it, most of them can. I need to find that one guy who can't be bought. I need to add him to my security team here on the streets of Anchorage and pair him up with my guy Dragonfly.

These people up here in Alaska are an enigma. They prance around when they talk about how long they have lived in this state, but I can't find a single guy who actually knows the streets of Anchorage. We had to bring in Dragonfly to lock it down for now.

My main business is flesh—I sell women. I need to keep the salmon running twenty-four hours a day for these predators out here; they have to eat. Someone is dipping their finger into my pie and killing some of my dancers. We need to figure this out and stop them cold.

Exotic dancers are going missing, and bodies are being found everywhere. This most definitely tends to put a crimp into a young woman's enthusiasm for the profession. It can also scare off legitimate customers. Right now all of these missing exotic dancers are hurting my business over on Fourth Avenue. We need to start getting eyes on our locations and beef up our security measures.

Right now I am having a big problem with my other associates from across the ocean. If I can't keep up with their demand, they are threatening me with some extremely unpleasant actions. I need to get several more people out there hunting for our main moneymaker—the babies and young girls.

The real money is young flesh—baby girls with blond hair and blue eyes who are one-and-a-half years old to two-and-a-half years old. The next level of profit is young girls with blond hair and blue eyes who are seven to eleven years old and are sexually unmarred. They are dream fulfillers.

Now I just need several guys with a big backbone who are looking to get wealthy. I am talking real wealth that can bring big life changes. I am talking about a lot of money beyond people's wildest dreams.

Is it possible to find true grit up here? Are there any real predators in Alaska? Is there anyone in this state willing to take big chances? Am I crazy for setting up shop in Anchorage? A bunch of hillbillies, every last one of them.

Fourth Glimpse
Dragonfly: Alaskan Hitman

Napa Valley, California, 1970s.
My mother warned me about them many times. What made me come here today?

My little brother Jimmy and I are crouched down peeking through the tall grass at a group of six older neighborhood kids about fifteen yards away. They are all known for being ruthless bullies, and we are very afraid of them.

All of them are standing around an old wooden apple bushel box, and their raucous laughter is carrying back to us with the blustery wind.

We watch as one of the bullies starts pouring liquid from a red gas can into the wooden apple crate. Suddenly the leader of the group, Billy, pushes him out of his way.

We watch while Billy lights a wooden match; the flame's flicker is glowing from his evil eyes. Without hesitating, Billy drops the burning match into the apple crate. With a big whoosh, flames of fury shoot up like a mushroom cloud. We can hear frantic screaming coming from the wooden crate; the sound of scritch-scratch is madly echoing out at us against the wind.

What we see is dreadful, tiny flaming kittens emerging, trying to jump out of the box. They are being consumed by flames and panic as they try to escape. All of the bullies have big sticks. They are using them to hit and push the kittens back into the opening of the fiery apple box.

My brother Jimmy is crying. His body is trembling with fear. With a tear-streaked face, he grimaces in horror while clutching at my leg.

Full of sadistic laughing and clapping, Billy starts pounding one of his buddies hard on his back while they celebrate their gruesome victory with jubilance.

Suddenly a flaming kitten falls screaming out onto the ground. I can see it twisting wildly as it cries from the pain of the fire; smoke is rising off its singed and blackened fur.

Overcome with fear, Jimmy and I bolt and start running down the path next to the railroad tracks trying to escape the cruelty we had just witnessed. I can hear the sound of the kitten's scream echoing in my mind as we run; their dying spirits are already reaching out to me from the great beyond.

Later that night I can hear my little brother Jimmy—he is crying on his lower bunk as he hunkers beneath me. Our mother's voice is softly consoling him. Jimmy responds by telling her he is afraid to die.

As I lay up here on my top bunk all alone nestled deep beneath my blankets, I have my sheets pulled tightly up over my head. I squeeze my pillow very tightly into a bear hug.

I can't help thinking that maybe a loving God doesn't exist in our world anymore. Are we all alone? Is there God? Does God love us? Do I love God? Does anyone care?

Fifth Glimpse
Milton Serrato: Alaskan Police Officer

Anchorage, Alaska, 1981.

What makes a person who enters law enforcement show a willingness to act dishonestly in return for money or personal gain? Have I not always done the right thing?

I would have never dreamed I could be impatiently waiting at a windswept trailhead for a depraved kidnapper and killer, but here I am delivering another package of flesh to him.

This girl was a fighter. I grabbed her last evening over by Mountain View. She quickly gave in to pressure when I told her I would arrest her and put her on a plane back down to the lower forty-eight states if she didn't come with me quietly.

We had fun. I made her tell me she liked what we were doing while I was raping her. When I started choking her, she started gurgling with a throaty noise that coaxed me into a subtle homicidal frenzy. Flushed with abhorrence, I realized it was not my sister Judy. I had already killed Judy down in Seward years ago.

When I killed my sister Judy, I felt unmanageable excitement. Lurid thoughts of wild behavior have clouded my mind ever since that day. Does this make me bad?

We grew up in Seward, Alaska, living on First Avenue. We used to ride our bicycles all the time along the winding Lowell Point Road. One day we parked our bicycles on the shoulder of the road along a very steep, sandy bluff. We decided to scurry up the slippery bluff so we could look out across Resurrection Bay. The wind was stiff at our backs, and it helped push us upward in our treacherous climb.

I quickly got above Judy by several hundred feet, and I decided to stop and rest by a very large boulder. When I placed my foot on the boulder, it was loose and wobbly. I curiously looked at my sister's downturned head as she struggled to gain her footing.

I never liked her. She is spoiled and thinks she is better than everyone. I lost my place at the center of attention when she was born thirteen years ago. It is time for me to regain my rightful place at the family table. As I start rocking the boulder with my foot, it moves very easily. Quizzically, Judy glances up at me.

I can see sweat is beading up on her forehead while she struggles to climb the banking. Judy with her long, blond hair and dark-green eyes has a curious look like "What are you doing, Milton? What's about to happen here?"

With all I have in me, I give the boulder one last big kick.

It starts tumbling and rolling haphazardly toward my sister Judy's upturned head. With a look of sheer terror on her face, she realizes what is about to happen to her. Suddenly the bouncing boulder impacts her head with a sickening thud. I can see Judy's body flailing helplessly as the boulder steamrolls over her.

Her limp body flops into a downward roll as the boulder trounces right over her and bounces down onto the street where it smashes into our bicycles and destroys both of them with a loud metallic crunching sound.

I can hear my sister's lonely whimpering for help off in the distance, the sound of her cries growing fainter now as the stiff wind carries them far away from me. I turn my back on my dying sister Judy. Her time has finally come. I did the right thing for everyone today. Thanks to me she will no more have a place at our family table.

Will my mother be happy? Did I gain my family's respect? Am I wrong for doing the right thing? Why do I feel so dirty? Should I be ashamed?

Chapter 1

US Army Private Anthony De Luciano

Fort Richardson, Alaska, 1981.

"De Luciano, you're coming with me."

"Yes, Sergeant." As we briskly walk downstairs to Commanding Officer Captain Waldrep's office, Sergeant Sidio starts explaining to me that I am being brought before a summary board of review for a possible nomination to Officers Candidate School in the near future. He tells me it is a great honor to even be considered.

When I am escorted into Captain Waldrep's office, I immediately recognize our Executive Officer Lieutenant McCrackin. I have never seen the two other officers before. They are both wearing battledress fatigues, with menacing sidearms enclosed in thick leather holsters. They each have piercing eyes as we go through our formal round of salutations.

After our formalities, Captain Waldrep speaks first. "Private De Luciano, this is CID investigator Ringo Covert and his partner CID investigator Jeremiah Johnson." *Huh, are these guys for real here? Jeremiah Johnson and Ringo*

Covert? What's going on here? Why am I standing here listening to this? CID? This can't be good for me, can it?

"Private De Luciano, General Masanotti and Lieutenant Colonel Palumbo have put you on a very short list of possible nominees to Officers Candidate School." This is mostly being based on your line scores on the ASVAB tests and the way you excelled in basic training."

My answer is succinct. "Sir, I would be honored."

CID investigator Ringo Covert speaks to me next. "De Luciano, you have a great opportunity here, right now. This is your time if you are willing to make the sacrifice. You ready, Private, for future glory?"

I am in a spot here, and I really can't say anything other than "Sir, I am ready. Yes, sir, send me."

All four of the officers look at each other, nodding. Then they all turn back to me. CID investigator Jeremiah Johnson speaks to me next. "Private De Luciano, you were tested in ten areas of knowledge. All of your scores are one hundred four to one hundred twenty-three; in six of the areas, you scored one hundred ten or above. That's amazing."

Lieutenant McCrackin speaks next. "Private De Luciano, I am going to be your main contact here in this unit. I have an open-door policy. You can counsel with me at any time of day or night. Is that understood?"

"Yes, sir, open-door policy." I need to ask the question that seems to be hanging in the room—"Lieutenant McCrackin, what is the actual mission, sir?"

Suddenly the room goes silent. Lieutenant McCrackin stands up and exits the office without speaking. CID investigator Jeremiah Johnson stands up and moves over in front of the office door as if he is guarding it against an intrusion or violent attack.

My body stiffens as CID investigator Ringo Covert motions for me to approach the Commanding Officer's desk. I stand up and walk over to Captain Waldrep's desk, while Investigator Covert is writing something on an orange piece of paper.

Captain Waldrep pushes the note to me as he speaks, "De Luciano, look at this address. It is for a small business in downtown Anchorage. Even though General Masanotti has not formally taken command of Fort Richardson yet, he is personally invested in this request."

I respond, "I understand, sir, and I appreciate the general's acknowledgment."

Investigator Covert takes the conversation over, goes into some details about the scope of the net we are casting, and gives all of us some big picture thinking. As he puts it, "Listen, we all need to be on the same page here, and that page is mine. Is that understood?"

Captain Waldrep, CID investigator Jeremiah Johnson, and I, Private Anthony De Luciano, all respond in unison, "Yes, sir."

"The United States has our eyes out to the horizon fifty years and beyond. Right now, all eyes are on Brezhnev. We have just been redirected by the Pentagon. Alaska is no longer our primary mission. We have been ordered to stand down and pull back, if necessary. The Pentagon has decided Alaska is no longer worth defending. We will be doing a joint-force mission with the Canadians north of Tetlin Junction to establish a rally point."

Now I need to admit this—at this point, I am getting very frightened by what I am hearing. No way. I joined the US Army to defend Alaska first and foremost. What are these guys telling me here? What am I listening to? Alaska no longer worth defending? Pull back? Where are we going? I have no idea what or where Tetlin Junction even is.

"De Luciano, this is where you come in. Our next major theater of operation is going to be Africa, and we have reason to believe our friends over at 417 D Street, Anchorage, Alaska, may have ties with South Africa."

Now I am totally confused. In basic training, we were training for El Salvador. Instead, I get reassigned, and they ship me north to Alaska. Now I am being told Africa is in my future. I just want to go fishing over at Ship Creek now; maybe somebody can pass me a cold drink, please. Africa sounds scary.

CID investigator Ringo Covert stops talking while he and CID investigator Jeremiah Johnson exchange places, and Investigator Jeremiah Johnson takes over the briefing from here. "OK, De Luciano, you can never ever mention Africa or South Africa to these friends of ours. Always let them lead you in those conversations if they come up. Got that?"

I shake my head as I respond, "Yes, sir, I will cooperate."

Investigator Johnson continues, "Great, next point then. You are now looking to become a drug dealer. You are a military presence wanting to be a force to be reckoned with on the streets of Anchorage. This will be your lead-in story. Is that clear?"

"Yes, sir."

Investigator Johnson explains further, "We need you to bring violence of action to the streets here for us. If you exemplify this, you will go far, De Luciano. Is that understood?"

"Sir, yes, sir."

Captain Waldrep speaks up, "De Luciano, we know you have never dealt drugs in your life. We know you have never been in the presence of drugs. We also know you can't be misdirected by contraband. This is why we will be giving you a clean slate during this mission. As things proceed, the proper misinformation will be leaked back through your chain of command, so, in the end, you will be indemnified, Private. Is that understood?"

"Yes, sir."

Captain Waldrep finishes, "Excellent. Now CID investigator Ringo Covert needs to speak with you alone, Private. Listen carefully to his words."

"Will do, sir."

Captain Waldrep and CID investigator Jeremiah Johnson both exit the office, leaving me alone with an extremely scary individual. He is large and menacing in stature, strapped, locked, and loaded with his military-issue sidearm on his hip.

"De Luciano, I am not your friend. I never have been. I never will be your friend. Is that understood, Private?"

"Yes, sir."

Covert continues, "I don't like people like you. I would strongly advise you not to like people such as myself. Is that understood?"

I retort, "Sir, yes, sir."

"You are now an animal, De Luciano. A predator in distress stalking the mean streets of Anchorage, Alaska, looking for his pack to encircle him. Is this understood, Private?"

"Yes, sir!"

"We will be watching you every step of the way out there. We will have eyes on you at all times. We want you to introduce yourself using the nickname you got in basic training. Will that be an issue for you, using the Stiletto as a street name for us?"

"No, sir."

Covert is looking at me very seriously. He shakes his head. "OK then, here it is, Private."

"No matter what you do, don't ever murder, kidnap, or rape anybody for these guys. If you are asked to engage in any of these illicit activities, you are to stand down immediately. It is imperative that you understand this point, Private De Luciano. Are we understanding each other right here, right now?"

"Yes, sir. Private De Luciano fully understands, sir."

Covert retorts, "Outstanding. Now get out of here and go be a private for one more night, and that's on my orders, soldier."

Chapter 2

Damon Dirks Prowls Among the Talus

Seward, Alaska, 1970s.

What am I looking for? Is there an answer to this, or are my actions the answer?

Miss Quintal keeps sending me messages. I like her smiles and the way she pushes on her hair in my presence. The other day she wore that very short skirt with tiny undies.

Did she knowingly open her legs? Did she want me to see her inner thighs? Is she just teasing me? Why would she provoke me to lust only to reject me?

Now I am tormented. Miss Quintal would never accept my sexual advances. It's not fair. She has all the power, with her long, luscious creamy-white legs, her experience, and an alluring position of authority. I need to take a hike out by Lowell Creek and think this through while I glass for sheep.

I recently bought a pair of used binoculars from my friend Milton. I could not pass them up. His father stole them from a campsite out along the Russian River last year. Then he gave them to Milton for his birthday, and Milton sold them to me for fifteen dollars. I felt it was an excellent deal between two good friends.

I want to be a business owner someday: Maybe I will own a small deli or bakery on a busy corner. Maybe I will combine them both, offering fresh baked goods with delicious pizza slices. Maybe I will learn to smile a little and try to fit in with my community.

I also want a family and to own a nice home. *Is that a funny thought? Me having a family? Me, Damon Dirks?*

I have despicable thoughts about nudity and gore. I may have even been born with a biochemical uniqueness according to my guidance counselor in junior high school. I guess that is a sad relief for the lurid images that flash through my sixteen-year-old mind.

In my dreams I can see Miss Quintal has her red dress on, and it is pulling up along her hip. I notice a small tear in her undies that seems frayed and uneven along the edges. I become overwhelmed with sudden and appalling depravity. Her hushed excitement in my presence is betrayed by her rosy red cheeks. Slowly my trembling bony fingers reach for her slender neck.

The sound of gravel crunching beneath my feet brings me back into the moment. I can hear the sound of Lowell Creek flowing over the gentle wind in the distance.

Over at our school there is a teachers' lounge that students are restricted from going into. Sometimes when I walk by, if the door is open, I can see Miss Quintal sitting on the couch. I have developed a small habit—I hesitate just long enough while lingering in the shadowy confine of the dusty hallway.

I am bedazzled by her voice as it sings out to me. While she is speaking with the other teachers, I can imagine her every move, seductive gestures freely offered in guidance.

We have a small computer room with three computers for students to use, which is adjacent to the teachers' lounge. The students' computer room has its own restroom, which makes it nice and private.

If you go into the computer room restroom and lock the door, you can stand up on the counter and push the ceiling tiles up out of the way. This lets you listen to what the teachers are talking about with a lot better clarity.

I am standing on the counter with the ceiling tile pushed back. I can hear Miss Quintal telling our social studies teacher, Mrs. Harriman, that she is hiking up into Lowell Canyon this coming weekend. She enjoys the hike out to the area over the little hill and around the big bend in Lowell Creek.

She explains to Mrs. Harriman that she brings a book and sunbathes near the cliffs' washout basin, among the big pile of rocks that accumulate at the base of the cliffs.

I know this area on the south side of Mount Marathon. I glass for sheep up in there with my new binoculars. I paced it out last time I went in a few days back. According to my stride length, it measures out to be about four thousand feet from the trailhead at the end of the road, less than a one-mile walk.

My plans are set for this coming Sunday morning. They are predicting clear, sunny sky, but up in Lowell Creek Canyon, the wind can howl for no reason at all with a tempestuous cloud-filled wailing.

I like to think of myself as a victorious wolf howling at the moon, a cunning predator scattering his prey. Each step I take is with purpose; every move you make I watch. All your sounds summon my hidden desire, the predator within prowls on a moonlit night.

I paced my hike this morning. It was exactly 1,334 paces to my ambush point among the talus.

I feel confident Miss Quintal will find her way here by midmorning. Tantalizing thoughts of her exposed flesh are all absorbing and burning in my mind. Engorged with lust, I find it difficult to stand up and walk.

Her bad manners have brought me here today, and now I am going to make her listen to my unheard feelings.

Is this the place to dig my hole? Will it go undetected? How do I keep animals away?

I have been reading a book on African occult. In Africa they like to dig their graves with the length orientated east–west, placing their victims in the hole laying on their sides with their feet pointing west.

They view their murder victims as animals, and animals always die on their sides. Human beings are usually laid to rest on their backs with dignity. So I dig a narrow grave where pretty little Miss Quintal can spend the rest of a bleak eternity laying on her side like the animal she has become to me.

I am starting to get groggy with the warmth of the rising sunshine. My ill-willed thoughts have continued to spiral. My mind becomes a mirror of malignant distortion when I see a person moving slowly along the trail coming my way.

I can see the person is wearing a lime-green hat, and they seem to be lost in thought. As they move over the small hill and around the bend, I can see it is Miss Quintal. She is all alone and walking due west toward my lurking shadow.

The cold chain feels good in my hands. As I work it gently and silently through my fingers, I become engorged with spineless perversions. I find myself standing on a jagged precipice. I am struggling to see if this is who I am, it seems like I am looking through a dark glass, but I have a strong need to see my face.

Is it too late for me? Was it only a matter of time before it came to this? Am I about to kill my first victim? Who is ready to pounce? Who am I right now? Am I a murderer? Is my name Damon Dirks?

A slight drizzle has begun to fall, and a light fog has enclosed us. Miss Quintal's eyes widened at the last moment when she sees me creeping toward her. Now she is wild eyed and struggling against my chain. I find myself disgustingly aroused at her pain, slightly amused that I will never release her.

Meet lady death, Miss Quintal. Now one last dance together. Then silence in the valley will be your muse. I twist the chain and hear a sickening sound like twigs snapping. One last shriek bellows like a low rumble from deep within her stomach.

I didn't realize how heavy her dead body would be. I took my time smelling her hair, inhaling her fragrance, and breathing in her dying spirit while whispering prayers to the sky gods of vengeance.

Her dainty necklace is tightly clasped in my cold bony fingers, when suddenly I become overcome with delight. I start dancing in small circles to an unheard beat while pounding on my chest and howling with the wind as the victorious wolf.

Like a skittish werewolf clawing back into the confinement of his hidden lair, I stand growling at the midmorning fog, hardened by a sudden lack of empathy.

Chapter 3

Snoopy's T-Shirt and Smoke Shop

417 D St, Anchorage, Alaska.

"Listen to me, Rat. Stop being so sloppy in here, will you? We need to tighten this ship up and fast. Get Dragonfly to stop by later today or early tomorrow morning. I have some things we need to discuss with him. Can you do that for me, or is it too much to ask?"

Rat responds, "No, man. It's good. He is already here like the wind, whoosh into the shadows."

Maestro retorts, "You are weird man—I mean weird. Why don't you think of getting off the peace pipe? That stuff will cloud your mind up."

Rat speaks up, "Maestro, my brother, a guy calling himself the Stiletto walked in here two days back looking to buy a small amount of herbal candy for his brain. These were his words when he walked in: 'Hey, my friend, do you have anything you can sell me for my brain?'"

Maestro inquires, "He asked for something for his brain?"

"Yes, I just knew he wasn't a cop asking like that."

Maestro gives Rat a curious, maybe even a quizzical, look, and responds, "No. I agree. No cop is going to walk in here and talk to you like that."

Rat continues, "I bring it up because he told me he wanted to take the streets of Anchorage with his fists. He told me he wanted to be the biggest drug dealer in Fort Richardson and Elmendorf AFB combined."

Maestro replies, "Sounds like we have some big aspirations going with this guy. Do you have his contact information? Also would your first impression be that this guy could back his big mouth up?"

Rat responds, "Yes to both questions."

Maestro nods and slowly walks over to the window with his hands clasped behind his back. He stands to look out at D St toward the intersection of W Fourth Avenue.

He nods toward Turf Paradise on the corner, a busy pool-hall type of establishment. "Do you think he can start by cleaning that mess up? Make the call. Let's see when he can be here to meet with me."

Rat immediately obeys, picks up the telephone, and dials out to Fort Richardson.

A loud voice booms through the telephone speaker. "56th Engineers, we are second to none. How may I direct your call?"

Rat greets the person and then explains, "I know this may sound a little strange, but a guy named Stiletto gave me this telephone number and told me I could contact him with it if I needed to speak with him."

The voice booms back, "Stiletto—you need to give me several minutes to round him up, but yes, he is available. Hold on, sir."

After several minutes: "This is the Stiletto. Who is this?"

"Hey, it's the Candy Man down at Snoopy's. Are you heading downtown anytime soon?"

Stiletto retorts, "Listen, I don't do candy. If you can put me onto some high test, I will be all in with that plan."

"OK. Try to cool down, man. It's all good here, you know. We just want you to stop by and meet the boss."

"OK, listen. You said your name was Rat. Are we still running with that?"

"Yes, I'm Rat. That's my name."

Stiletto continues, "OK, Rat, set it up for me. How should I dress? Am I coming to the store, or are we going to meet somewhere else?"

Rat responds, "No. Just come here to the store at 417 D St. Give me a day and time. The sooner the better for everyone. We are here now if you could be here."

"I am just heading over to the bus stop now. I need to stop off in Muldoon at the Gun Trader Shop first, though. Is that OK with you guys?"

Rat replies, "Yeah, sure. If you can be here before one p.m., that would be great. Maestro can't wait to meet you. He is looking at me right now, so do your best to be here, man. Don't let us down."

Stiletto closes it out, "See you two guys in about ninety minutes."

The People Mover bus rolls to a stop on W Fifth Ave just past D St. I get off the bus in front of Club Paris restaurant. I hear they sell great food and frozen White Russians to fight for.

It is a very quick walk over to Snoopy's T-Shirt Shop, but I linger back for several moments to mull a few things over.

I mean, am I insane here? What am I doing? How can I take the streets with my fists? Anyone can fight—I hit you, and you then hit me; look it's a fight. Am I working for CID? Or am I working with CID? Does CID even know who I am? Is the general aware of this mission? Did CID lie to me? Have I ever met with CID?

Two big bells tied to the door of 417 D St snap me back into the moment as I step into the shadowy interior of the T-Shirt Shop.

A loud horn ringing from a pinball machine in the back of the arcade area causes me to look down through several racks of tie-dyed T-shirts and sweatshirts at a group of young guys staring intently down at the machine one of their friends is playing. The wall above their heads is adorned with black-light posters and large pictures of all the current rock-and-roll gods that rule our world.

Over at the front counter, Rat is showing two women a water pipe that he is calling the rose. His long, shaggy hair is tied back with a thin black headband. He is wearing a pastel tie-dyed T-shirt with a peace symbol emblazoned across the front. Both women are nervously giggling at his comments.

Rat looks over at me and then nods over toward the cash register area. I follow his eyes, and I watch as an older gentleman, who is well dressed, makes some change for a lone customer standing at the register.

This has to be Maestro; this is the man. This is a big-time organized crime crew right here. Don't mess this up, Stiletto. Don't flinch with these guys, or you will probably be dead.

Maestro has sharp-cut white hair, and his mustache is well trimmed.

He is wearing a crisply pressed blue button-down shirt with the cuffs rolled back a little bit. His gold watch is encrusted with diamonds. When I look back up, I can see the glittering of diamond flecks embedded in the frames of his eyeglasses.

Hiding behind his expensive glasses, but not afraid to see what's in the room, are a set of steel-blue eyes with laser-like focus.

I hold my hand out to shake his hand, but he ignores me. He looks over at Rat, and with a menacing growl, he bellows, "Rat, throw everybody out of here and lock the door. Tell them to come back in an hour and you will refund any money we owe them for their games."

Maestro spins toward me, "You . . . Stiletto . . . follow me. Keep your mouth shut until we get into my office."

I silently follow Maestro through a maze of clothes racks loaded with T-shirts. We pass into a small, very dark arcade area with about fifteen assorted games. All the way in the back, we come to two locked doors. One is for his office.

I wait while he struggles with the keys to unlock the door. I can hear him muttering under his breath about how he can't find any good help.

Once we step inside, he points over toward a chair for me to sit in, while he sits upon the desk. Maestro rests his chin on his hand as if he is deep in thought while looking down at me for several moments before speaking, "Stiletto, do you smoke marijuana?"

I respond, "Yeah, sure, on occasion, if it's available to me."

Maestro retorts, "I like that answer. Well, it's available right here, my friend," while he is leaning down to open a bottom drawer in the desk.

"I don't know how to roll a joint, so you will have to do the honors for us, Stiletto. Everything that you need is in this box."

Maestro watches every move I make with laser-like precision. His eyes follow every shadow being cast from the yellowing incandescent light bulb hanging above our heads for what may lurk.

I feel like this guy is unsure about me. He is watching me like a hawk. I need to be steady, just smoking a little herb with the boss man here. I am just following orders, making friends, meeting and greeting. Don't mess this up, Stiletto.

"Why do they call you Stiletto . . . Stiletto?" Maestro sarcastically asks me.

I exhale the smooth cannabis smoke up toward the light bulb while handing him the burning marijuana cigarette. "Because I was able to dominate with the pugil sticks in basic training."

Maestro responds, "What are pugil sticks? Please explain them to me while we smoke."

"A pugil stick is a heavily padded pole-like training weapon used by the military in training for rifle and bayonet combat. The pugil stick is similar to a Japanese bo, and sometimes it might be marked to indicate which end represents the bayonet and which the rifle butt."

Maestro is nodding while he takes his glasses off. "Are you a bad boy, Stiletto?"

"No, sir, Maestro, just a good fighter."

Maestro smiles and pats me on my shoulder. "I love that answer; now follow me up to the front of the store please, and leave that joint in the ashtray for me to smoke later."

I follow Maestro back up through the winding maze of clothes racks to the front counter area. Rat has a curiously sad look on his face as if he got left out of the good times in the back room. I just brush his despondent attitude off with a grin.

Maestro calls me over to the storefront window, and he puts his arm around my shoulders, "Stiletto, look at that big mess over on the corner of W Fourth Avenue and D St. It's because of that dive Turf Paradise. What would you do to clean something like that up if it was on your front doorstep?"

I step back out of his embrace. "What would I do? Watch this."

As I am walking out of the front entrance of Snoopy's T-Shirt and Smoke Shop, I remove the black leather belt I am wearing, and I start rolling it up onto my right fist so the belt buckle is on top of my knuckles pointing out toward the enemy.

I quickly approach a group of five guys standing on the corner and swigging from a crumpled brown paper bag. One of the guys looks over toward me and yells out, "What are you looking at, soldier boy?"

I run and jump in with a straight punch to his face. His red bulbous nose explodes into a salty spray of crimson that splashes back onto his companion's jackets, and here we go.

A furious melee ensues as we all skirmish on the sidewalk of W Fourth Avenue. One of the guys smashes me over the head with the bottle they had been drinking from, and I buckle to the ground. Suddenly another guy runs in with a knee that hits my left shoulder.

I stand up and connect with a solid uppercut that drops a second guy to the ground. He crawls over and lays against a parked car. The guy who hit me with his knee turns and tries to punch me behind my head, but he swings wide.

I counter with an uppercut to his stomach, which doubles him over onto his knees, I jump up in the air and come down with a sidekick to his face, sending his head slamming into the sidewalk with a sickening thud.

The other two guys are visibly frightened. Stumbling over each other, they start running and screaming, "You're crazy. You're crazy!"

I start screaming and pounding on my chest, "I am the Stiletto. I will fight anybody in Anchorage! I own these streets now. Tell all your friends I am coming to get them. I'll fight the whole town. I'm the Stiletto. I'm coming to fight all of you! Here I come!"

W Fourth Avenue grows eerily quiet all around me. The crowd that had gathered has now dispersed into nearby taverns and pubs. My homicidal frenzy has me frothing at the mouth and ready to pounce like a wolf.

I look over to Snoopy's, and I can see Maestro standing on the sidewalk frantically waving for me to get back to his store. I break into a run across D St. Fighting gets your adrenaline going, so my body is flush with a sudden surge of excitement.

When I get back into the store, Maestro tells Rat to lock the door again and has both of us follow him back to his office.

Both guys are expressing an overwhelming exuberance at what they witnessed me doing. Maestro is telling me he has never seen a street fight like that in his life before. "Stiletto man, that was some stuff. Where did you learn to fight like that?"

I reply, "Both of my grandfathers boxed at an amateur or semi-pro level, and they always showed me things while growing up. My father was a known street fighter in our area. He was ruthless, from what I have been told."

Maestro retorts, "I guess the lessons paid off, because that was some top-notch happenings out there. I can use a guy like you."

I respond, "OK, like what would you want me to do for you?"

Maestro looks at Rat. Rat lights the remainder of the joint that is in the ashtray, before Maestro speaks again.

"Are you a cop?"

Confused, I reply, "Huh . . . a cop, are you trying to offend me, man?"

Maestro smiles, "I love you already, Stiletto. I love you already."

I speak up, "Listen, Maestro, I ain't no cop, never have been, never will be, lose that with me."

Maestro retorts, "Wow, Stiletto has a pair. OK, Stiletto, can you sell quantity?"

I hesitate before responding, "Quantity? Quantity of what?"

Maestro shakes his head. "Are you going to make me spell it out for you?" while he taps his gnarly finger against my forehead.

My eyes go wide. My mouth is hanging partially open. There might even be a little bit of sweat beading up on my forehead. "No, no need to spell it out for me, Maestro. Sorry, I just try not to say it unless we actually need to say it."

Maestro is slightly smiling. "I like that. I like that concept of only saying what needs to be said."

Suddenly, and without warning, Maestro grabs me and slams me against the wall. My head impacts the wall with a violent thud. Grimacing while tightly clenching his teeth, Maestro growls, "Don't you ever mess with me, Stiletto. Don't you ever, ever mess with me. Is that understood?"

Before I can answer him, he screams, "Don't make me send Dragonfly after you. Dragonfly will break you in two and toss your cold, limp body into Cook Inlet."

Rat is standing behind Maestro. His cold dead eyes are looking right through me while he shakes his head back and forth. He slices a line across his throat with his fingers and then winks at me over Maestro's shoulder.

Maestro slaps my face. "Look at me, Stiletto. Look into my eyes. You see these eyes? These eyes see you now, understood? Understood?"

I tell Maestro what he wants to hear. "Absolutely, yes. Loud and clear, Maestro."

Maestro relaxes, and casually looks over toward Rat. "OK, you two guys are working together from now on. When you need anything, contact Rat first, OK?" He continues, "OK, now I also want you to work with Dragonfly. Rat is going to set that meeting up for you."

"Listen to me, Stiletto. Dragonfly is a nasty degenerate killer. Always try to stay on his good side just to be safe, understood?"

Chapter 4

Dragonfly: The Degenerate Hitman

Government Hill, Anchorage, Alaska, 1981.

Dragonfly has been crying and talking to me for about fifteen minutes now. A soft drizzle has started to fall, and I can hear a low rumble growling in my aching stomach.

"Stiletto, my Little Monkey, I have deteriorated physically, mentally, and morally in the last two years, man. Maestro has me doing some very bad and horrific deeds out here. I could be a walking billboard for ACDC's *Dirty Deeds Done Dirt Cheap* album. I get no respect from anyone accept for you, Stiletto. No one in Anchorage loves me. No one around here wants me in their business—no really they just tolerate me, Stiletto, man."

In the short time I have known Dragonfly, he has never shown me any bad manners unless you consider threatening to kill me close to twenty times to be bad manners. That's just him talking tough because he likes to stay hidden behind his gray emotional mask of ice-cold steel that he carries around with him.

The drizzle is turning into a steady rain now. The cadence of the raindrops pelting off Dragonfly's orange taxi is somehow relaxing me.

Dragonfly continues to speak, "I feel like a depraved animal. Everyday violence and rage drive my machine. I scare off every woman I try to date. I even had to kill four or five of them. It gets messy, Stiletto."

My stomach lurches. Dragonfly's words have caused uncontrolled movement in every part of my body, but I hold steady. His black eyes seem to be blazing holes through the back of my head.

I knew he could be violent, but I am sensing a deeper, smoldering type of anger in this guy. He is the type of killer who is going to hold it all in until he explodes, becoming homicidal, frenzied, and out of control at the moment of truth.

"Little Monkey, just this year my birthday got ruined on me, man. I was seeing a girl named Chrissy, and you will never guess what she tried to give me for a birthday present. Go ahead. Try to guess."

His look of inquiry is serious. He wants an answer from me, so I give it a whirl. "Let me guess. A green T-shirt and a black bandana?"

Dragonfly sarcastically replies, "Wow close, but no! No, that could have worked for me, but she gave me a red necktie!"

While it may be a little strange to think someone would see Dragonfly as a tie guy, I have to admit I am not able to understand the problem. Maybe she just wants to improve his wardrobe and his self-esteem?

"Stiletto, so I let it slide for a while, just let it go, you know, man? We started partying. Our glow was growing by the moment. Then this psycho has the guts to ask me if I like my necktie!" His head violently snaps in my direction.

"Stiletto, my friend, please don't ever make me have to kill you. I love you, man. Listen to me, Stiletto. You're my only family, kid. I am giving you permission to use my name out here on the streets of Anchorage. Are we good, Stiletto?"

Dragonfly has tears dripping off his nose. Blotches of red cover his big bald head as he looks down at me. "I had to kill her, man. What kind of a question is that—do you like your necktie?"

"Do I like my necktie? Try this one on for size, Chrissy. Chrissy, do you like my necktie? I drove her down to Beluga Point and tossed her into Cook Inlet. I used to love sitting in there watching the sunset, but now she went and ruined that experience for me also."

Dragonfly drones on. His voice is buzzing in and out of my mind as I ponder his last words.

Is this guy sitting here confessing to me about murdering his girlfriend Chrissy? He was clear; how do I wrap my head around this? Did this guy kill a woman because he didn't like her birthday present? Now he is telling me she ruined one of his favorite pullout spots to watch sunsets? I mean cursed be Beluga Point, how dare you.

Dragonfly smacks my shoulder. "Stiletto, you have my phone number. If anyone, and I mean anyone, in this town or state ever mess with you, call me immediately, OK?"

"It's my house out here. I make my own rules, understood? If you need a ride anywhere, call me, I drive a taxi for a living, or at least that's our background story around Anchorage. Do you know what I mean?"

I assure Dragonfly I know what he means by telling him, "I will call for an orange taxi, and I will tip the driver well, my friend."

He finally relaxes and grins a little bit and gently pats me on my left shoulder with his mitt-size sweaty hand. "You and I are going to be very good friends, Stiletto. Just don't make me have to kill you, my friend."

Chapter 5

Milton Serrato: Mischievous Police Officer

Unknown location in Anchorage, Alaska.

A mischievous allegation for which there is not a shred of evidence has recently been cast against me by the community and my coworkers.

An informal and anonymous complaint was filed against me, stating that I was lingering over at Dirk's Bakery while on duty and that I was a disgrace to the uniform.

It went on to further imply that the owner, Damon Dirks, and I have been involved with after-hours gambling establishments in and around the city of Anchorage.

I have always done the right thing. I became an Alaskan police officer to continue doing the right thing. Even back in Seward, I did the right thing. My mother allowed Judy to disrupt our family tree. My mother should have ended that pregnancy. She mismanaged her body and her family; my mother didn't do the right thing. She laid that burden on me, her son

Milton. She hung a weight around my neck and pushed me into a spiraling future filled with nothing but fearful futility.

I walked out of my house last night cold and disheveled, feeling exhausted as if I was fighting for each step. I forced myself to report for duty. Now they have me patrolling over near Fairview, along E Ninth Avenue. It seems like they are testing me to see if I will stop in over at Dirk's Bakery.

Not this morning. I already met with Damon out on Arctic Valley Road. There is a pullout just before the pavement ends on your left; we meet in there. There are some transformers there for the District Utility Plant and a trail that follows out along the powerline, so it is easy to locate and follow in the dark of night.

Damon likes to walk out and glass for sheep here. When I come up over the hill and around the bend, I quickly flash my cruiser's blue lights. It is amazing how far the light carries up into the mountains and beyond. If he is already at his truck, he will do three quick flashes of his headlights to signal me of his presence.

I delivered him a pretty little package. I helped him load her onto his transport wagon. She had long auburn hair, green eyes, and luscious, long lashes. I picked her up on the Boniface Parkway. She was hitchhiking in front of Carpentier's Lounge. At first, she was hesitant to get into my cruiser, but Lucky Lucy, my .357 revolver, can be a very persuasive partner indeed.

Debbie got in, and we had some fun. She told me how much she loves me. She told me I was the best lover she ever got with. She didn't have a choice, I mean not really. I made her scream it to me, scream how sexy I am while I was gently choking her.

I was feeling like a monster getting ready to bite. The exhilaration and arousal I felt when I tore her undies off her was undeniably satiating. I didn't realize how tantalizing engaging in disrespectful behavior could be. Has society force-fed me a malignant distortion of their reality?

My actions from last night have me feeling like I am a dead man walking. I have a nagging thought that a hangman is waiting for me at the gallows pole. I can hear the judge's greasy gavel pounding, now rusty prison doors grinding, creaking, and slamming closed.

You don't know who I am, but I am watching what you are doing. The grim reaper seems to follow my every move now, keeping death's shadow bristling right at my door.

Chapter 6

The Raucous Ravens of No Man's Land

Arctic Valley Road, Anchorage, Alaska.

Our mission is Alaska Primary—we are the boys already deployed who will hold this ground. Arctic Valley with the missile site is ours to defend.

The primary security for Arctic Valley Road is assigned to Second Platoon of the Fifty-Sixth Engineers, from the front gate of Fort Richardson up through the Moose Run Golf course area and beyond.

Most civilians are afraid to venture beyond the power utility plant because of the high-frequency live-fire exercises being conducted on Fort Richardson at this time. Many times when we walk into a local business, we get asked this question: "What are you guys doing up there in the valley? It sounds like the end of the world up there."

The District Utility Plant is almost three miles from the front gate of Fort Richardson. When you are executing security sweeps, a three-mile patrol can take four, maybe even five, hours to complete in one direction.

This area is affectionately known as No Man's Land. As you clear the perimeter of the utility plant, there is a small dirt parking area on the left-hand side of the road with a powerline trail that runs out from it. The powerline has utility poles running along the east side of the trail.

Arctic Valley Road is paved up to this point, and as we start approaching this area, we can see a large flock of raucous ravens jumping all around in treetops along the road on the same side as the utility plant. I am on point with the M60 machine gun, so I am the first soldier in line.

As we crest the little uprise on the corner, I can see a blanket of ravens that sweeps down to the corner of the utility plant. The ravens are perched on a chain-link fence, easily two hundred or maybe even three hundred ravens all looking at the same spot beneath them.

As my platoon starts to catch up with me, someone comments that there must be a moose kill down in the treeline that the ravens are sitting on. Everyone is anxious to move along. Someone yells out, "Stiletto, let's move them out . . . the hair is standing up on the back of my neck in here." As we slowly start to move out, none of the ravens even flinch.

Hundreds of ravens silently peer at us while we walk by them, accompanied by gravelly crunching footsteps echoed eerily from beneath heavy mountain boots. Our dusty faces are sweating under black-and-gray camouflage. The salt from the sweat is stinging our eyes. Nervously, we intently stare back at them.

They stay tight to whatever is attracting them to this spot. Their shiny feathers are bristling as they silently wait for us to pass. As we pass through the gauntlet of ravens, I am filled with unsettled thoughts—chilling, ominous.

When we move back down through the area several hours later, many of the ravens are on the ground below the roosting flock in the trees. Each individual raven is hopping up and down, loudly squawking, while many of them are scratching and pecking at the ground.

We can hear their talons raking at the grass and leaf debris that litters the ground beneath them. They are picking and prodding like prospectors at some unknown buried treasure. Gruesome is the only thought that comes into my mind.

Later that night I find myself tightly clutching at my pillow while waking up in a cold sweat. I am trembling with fear at the thought of what attracted that large flocks of ravens we saw today. Their chilling cries gravely echoing throughout the windy valley keep calling me back in my head.

My weeping eyes have followed along a rusty barbed wire fence on the edge of No Man's Land, while many a raven "kraa" kept scratching at my heart. Their profane burial didn't bring them eternal rest, nor could the midnight fires ease their primal fear.

Chapter 7

CID Identifies Stiletto to Maestro

417 D St, Anchorage, Alaska.

Tonight, all I want to do is drink a few cold beers with my friends Bryone and Lamps.

I can look out my barracks' window and see the District Utility Plant from here. The flocks of ravens are still up there circling, following an invisible draft like a black funnel cloud dancing on a stormy horizon.

We need to go back up into No Man's Land and investigate. Ravens don't just hang tight to one location like that. They are scavengers. They move from one opportunity to the next. *Unless there is a constant food source available. Why haven't they moved on yet? We are talking about hundreds of ravens. There has to be a lot of food available for them.*

I find the bus ride from Fort Richardson out through Muldoon onto Tudor Road to be very relaxing as the bus moves in its own slow, heavy, awkward way toward the busy, noisy downtown Anchorage area.

When we get to Club Paris, the bus lurches as the driver shifts it into park, and a few people stumble and almost fall from the swaying motion. A fierce wind whips my face as I step from the warmth of the bus. The compression from the bus engine blasts hot exhaust into my face as I walk by the smoking tailpipe.

I walk in on the middle of Maestro's tirade while he angrily scolds Rat. Rat seems to be slightly agitated by the shouting. I hesitate for a few seconds at the front door, not wanting to get caught eavesdropping.

Maestro stares over at me, then spits with venom onto the carpet of the store. He looks back at me and screams, "De Luciano, keep walking to the back of the store. Don't you mess with me, De Luciano, and keep your mouth shut."

OK, how does he know my real name? Should I turn and run out of here? What have I got myself into now? Is CID behind this? Is Maestro about to kill me? Will Rat watch?

Maestro gives me a disgusted glance over his right shoulder, then spins around, yelling at Rat. "Rat, lock the door and keep an eye out. Don't let anyone see you. Stay hidden out here, but keep the door locked, no matter what happens."

As I weave my way through overloaded clothes racks filled with tie-dyed T-shirts, the pungent scent of spicy incense wafts lazily through the damp, musty interior of the store.

When I get to the back area of the store, the office door is open, so I step in, but I stay standing up while pushing my back firmly against the wall.

Maestro storms in, scowling and muttering obscenities. "CID was in here. Who are you? I need to know who you are. Tell me who you are. Why was CID asking me about my relationship with you?"

I retort, "What do you mean CID? Forget CID. Maybe you are working with CID. I walk in here, and you start talking CID. I have to wonder myself."

Maestro rolls up his sleeves and puts his hands on his hips. "Two CID investigators dressed in monkey suits were in here, warning us about you." They tried to scare me off dealing with you."

I reply, "Listen, forget CID. They are not my friends. CID walked into your business talking big words. Why are we going to let them push us around?"

Maestro steps right up into my face. He spits against the wall next to my head. "Stiletto, are you trying to make a monkey out of me? I ain't no monkey, I ain't no monkey, Stiletto. There are plenty of low-level people in this town trying to take me for their monkey."

I understand his feelings and try to reassure Maestro. "Maestro, I will pound the first CID officer I see just for you, my friend. You point him out and watch my hams-for-fists go to work and turn his chin into a splatter of gristle."

Maestro seems dumbfounded by my words. Speechless, he motions for me to approach him. He firmly grabs my face with both of his slimy hands and kisses me on my sweaty forehead. Then he embraces me and tells me I am the son he never had.

"Stiletto, you're like the son I never had."

Chapter 8

Damon Dirks Hunts the Wild Cherry

E Fourth Avenue, Anchorage, Alaska.

She is sitting in front of me with her mouth partially open, wide baby blue eyes, and sweat dripping off her nose. She seems unfazed by her nudity.

When I had stepped into this shadowy confine, she was dancing and writhing to a beat at another table. When she had finished, a subtle head nod from me brought her scurrying over to my table. "Hi, my name is Patty. What are we doing for you over here tonight?"

"Patty, they call me Leroy. I will pay you one dance to sit down at my table and listen to my proposal for you to make some money. Do you want to sit with me and talk about making money, Patty?"

Patty replies, "I sure do. Let me hear this extravagant money-making plan of yours, Leroy. Maybe we can run away together someday into the sunset?"

Her response has piqued my curiosity along with my carnal desires. She might be the one I have been looking for. "Patty, you don't look like you want to dance in a place like this forever. You have the physical attributes to be a model. Have you ever thought of modeling, Patty?"

With a sheepish grin, she responds, "Being in front of a camera would make me feel very uncomfortable for some reason. Maybe because once the photo image is captured, everyone can see your defects more clearly, and it's forever. No, I never really thought about modeling at all."

"Well, listen, Patty, I am willing to help you out in any way I can. I am an aspiring photographer. I will do a photo shoot for you in the privacy of my own home. We will be alone so you can be more relaxed during the photo session."

"As you know, one of the biggest hurdles for any young model is building her photo portfolio. It can be very expensive, and the agencies can be extremely picky. I know what they want, and I know what they don't want, Patty."

Patty speaks up, "How am I making money during this? I told you I am not looking to become a model."

"Well, Patty, here's the answer to that question. I am going to pay you three hundred dollars for your time, and you get a full set of the photos to start your modeling portfolio platform, plus you gain the experience of doing a photo shoot."

She looks up at me. Her curiosity is there. I can see it in her eyes.

Now I have her in my snare. Familiar words are about to be spoken. Listen for it, and here it comes. "What do you get? Are you looking for sex? I don't do that. I am a dancer only. That's what I do. I dance erotically and seductively for money." *And I have her; she is all mine.*

"Patty, I am married, and I am a business owner; discretion is assured. I am not looking to cheat on my wife; that's just not me. I am looking to start a side business of erotic and sensual photography for professional women and men in the adult entertainment industry. Listen, my time with you is up for now, but here is a phone number to contact me. If you call, it will be fun, quick, and easy. The easiest three hundred dollars you will ever make in your life, Patty."

Little twerp! Thinks he can come in here and just buy me outright? Should I be flattered by his offer? Should I consider being a model? No, I am too fat; my thighs look like hams. I would shatter his camera lens into a thousand pieces. The poor pathetic guy thinks I am modeling material; still, I have to wonder. Should I call him? He wouldn't hurt a flea? Would he?

The US military has been increasing the frequency of their live-fire maneuvers. This closes the airspace down over the two military bases: Elmendorf AFB and Fort Richardson. This means I have to get tower clearance to use the airspace, thereby leaving a record of my flights. I can't allow that to happen.

This is one of my favorite spots in Anchorage. No one knows who owns it, so they call it No Man's Land. I set a tree stand up for observation about a half-mile up the trail along the powerline. I was able to find a large cottonwood tree among some Sitka spruce to place it in.

It gave me a great panoramic view of the Chugach frontal range in here. Looking up through the valley toward Temptation Peak, I often see Dall sheep up on these mountain peaks wandering lazily about their business.

I have a lawn wagon hidden up at the trailhead to haul my women in with. I stood all my digging tools up against a few trees when I completed digging her grave so they will not get weathered as badly—this helps keep them preserved for my future digs.

It will also keep me from being seen and detected with tools—that would cause serious curiosity that no one needs right now. Maestro will send Dragonfly to my store if I screw up one more time—that is not a good situation for my family.

I have become involved with some despicable animals. They are stone-cold killers. Now I am beholden to them for saving my business and enriching my life. I feel dejected lately as if nothing in my life matters anymore. I have nobody to help me out of this. I just keep spiraling.

I am standing on the District Utility Plant's powerline trail looking directly west into the setting sun. It is being filtered through spruce boughs laden with wind chimes and dream catchers, and I am shaking like a leaf.

This is my power spot in Anchorage. I own this ground. It is mine to hoard and protect from curious eyes. Hidden all through here, buried among the moss, lay hidden gems, my Saturday night specials, the sleeping ladies of Anchorage's midnight sun.

Chapter 9

Can Leroy (Damon) Come Out to Play?

No Man's Land, Anchorage, Alaska.

The wind can howl through these streets for no reason at all. I am standing with my back against a cold wall, realizing that city streets offer little pity for people like me.

I had to make the phone call to Leroy. I need the three hundred dollars to pay my rent this month, or my sister Ginny will throw one of her colossal temper tantrums. Dealing with her massive emotions can be tiring, to say the least. She is wearing me out. I am mentally exhausted and dejected by her.

Leroy gave me an address of 264 Muldoon Rd to meet him at the Cabin Tavern. It's been here for a long time. Crumpled, dirty, grimy dollar bills adorn support columns over near the bar. One dilapidated pool table sits unevenly over in a dusty corner. It is shadowed by flickering neon light.

He told me to sit facing the front parking lot and that he would blink his headlights three times to signal me when he was here. It seems simple enough. Three blinks.

I just thought of this—one blink of his headlights for every one hundred dollars he is paying me. That is so adorable. I love him to death already. Will he like my body? He already saw me without my clothes on; was he disgusted? I am disgusted with me. I can't seem to escape being around myself. Who would want pictures of a deranged rosy-cheeked blonde?

My face is bruised from being battered by Leroy. His animosity has been shockingly severe. His pounce was full of perversion. His sexual behavior with me would be considered abnormal even for a depraved minded deviant.

It is pretty late out because we have total darkness for this time of year, but the surrounding woods are lit up by Leroy's fire. He has me chained to a tree by my neck with a dog leash. My vocal cords are paralyzed from hours of screaming into nothingness for his mercy. All I can do is moan now, but just barely. This seems to satisfy the beast.

I can see Leroy silhouetted against the flames of his roaring inferno as it threatens to ignite the surrounding forest down. He seems to be ritualistically dancing naked around the fire with nothing but his boots and glasses on. *Is he mocking me?*

I can hear a wind chime ringing in the background. Growling like a mad dog, Leroy turns and jumps on me again. His hard, black eyes radiate evil. I can't believe how frightened I am by his antics.

Usually, I am not afraid of anybody. I can take them all. Am I going to die tonight? Why did I call him? Is he going to release me? Is he just amusing himself with my pain? He seems to be mimicking my dance routine. Is Leroy dancing with my moves for me?

* * *

Patty's dying eyes are turning gray now, wild eyed. She seemed surprised that I didn't release her at the last minute. I can hear her feet bustling in the leaves as she strides across to the underworld, her one last dance with mother nature. Sounding like the pitter-patter of little feet, she attempts to scamper away from me across the blanket of cool moss beneath her dying body.

Honestly, the experience wasn't what I expected, and she didn't put up much of a fight. Was there any satisfaction at all? Am I that hardened by a lack of empathy? What am I looking for in a relationship? Just nothing, no reward for my efforts? How can people expect me to be happy? I might just as well give myself up to Dragonfly now. Let him put me out of my misery once and for all. It's just a matter of time anyway.

Let me gently remove her anklets and her waist chain. Then I will put her clothes back on for her burial. I also like to make a small incision along the spine where I cut out a small chunk of the backstrap, maybe six ounces of meat, to roast over my dwindling embers.

They say you are what you eat. If that is an accurate conclusion, then Patty will live on within my yearning and spineless soul forever.

Chapter 10

The Fly Visits Totem Theater

3131 Muldoon Road, Anchorage, Alaska.

Maestro called me, and now I have to jump for him. I can't even joke around about how high he wants me to jump because I might not like what he suggests I do with myself.

The short of the story is some desperado pulled into Anchorage thinking he will go outside of Maestro and make a name for himself flooding the streets with cheap cocaine.

Maestro will not be made a monkey out of, not in this man's town. The last person you ever want on your scent is Maestro. This guy is a stone-cold killer. Maestro is ruthless; leaning back in his overstuffed chair with steepled fingers, his withering looks of superiority can cause whiplash while you pull your head away trying to avoid his piercing hard eyes.

People need to understand out here on the streets if Maestro calls me I get angry. I know it doesn't seem fair, but it's the way it is. Now you are going to make me have to kill you for two reasons. Why? Why would you do this to yourself?

Maestro smacks me on my head with his bony knuckles and breaks me out of my daydream.

"Are you with me, Dragonfly? This kid Tommy can't just walk into Alaska like some wild-eyed mountain man stumbling around in a dry creek bed. Are you following me, or are you still thinking about that no good whore you have been shacking up with lately?"

"What is it with you and Rat? You guys both lack discipline. I can't find any good help in this trash bowl from Chugiak down to Girdwood. I need to pack it up and move to Miami. I can't believe you guys."

Maestro continues his tirade, "One more thing, you need to learn to dress right. You wouldn't embarrass your mother like this, would you? Well, would you? Answer me, Dragonfly, or I'll give a good swift kick to your behind."

Stammering, I respond, "No, Maestro, I wouldn't embarrass my mother like this, man. Come on, stop being so hard on me. I need to concentrate."

Maestro angrily retorts, "What do you need to concentrate on? What is so important going through that mind of yours?"

Without hesitation, I reply, "Tommy, 3131 Muldoon Road, Totem Theater. Theater Two. Front row, left-hand side. When I enter the theater from the main entryway, walk down and sit in the row of seats behind him, three seats to his right-hand side."

Maestro nods approvingly. "Tell him your name is Jethro. Don't worry about it. He has never talked with or set eyes on Jethro. His backpack will need to go with you after the dirty deed is done. Take the buy money and get it back to me after you scrape your share off the top, understood? Understood? Scrape your share off and rake it back to the dogs."

I reply, "I enjoy live entertainment, you know that, Maestro man. It speaks to who I am as a person. I like to get down and dirty, but going forward, on your advice, I will learn to dress better before I kill again, just for you, my friend, OK?"

Maestro condescendingly sneers at me, "Always the wise guy, Dragonfly, always running off with your mouth. If you would learn to keep your mouth shut, you would go far in this town. Just learn to keep your mouth shut."

The thing Maestro doesn't understand is these things never go as planned. No matter how many times I have told him this, it just doesn't seem to sink into his head. Look at him ranting and raving as if he is the mad dog. I am the killer, not him. Why do I put up with him and his abusive manners? Why am I working for a rabid wolf unleashed?

"Maestro, I got this man. Tommy walks no more. Trust me, he is dead already. Now I just need to go deliver the message to him in person. Trust me, he will understand our position when my interview with him is over."

This guy is driving me insane. He just stays on me no matter what I do, or don't do. *When do I kill him? Maybe it's time for Maestro to get snuffed? Maybe it's time for me to break Maestro in two and toss him into Cook Inlet?*

Muldoon offers no pretense, that's for sure. Totem Theater was built on one of the best vantage points in the city, offering gripping views of the Chugach mountains from the safety of its heavily cracked and frost-heaved parking lot.

We are told Tommy usually meets his guys here. Tonight I am Jethro, looking to expand my drug turf and bring in one or two new dealers. Tommy needs more product, and our story is we can supply him with an endless product, but Maestro and his strong-arm Dragonfly must never find out about it.

All I need Tommy to do is admit to me that he is willing to work behind Maestro's back. Once he walks into that trap, I have him, with no remorse. *If this kid is willing to come into Anchorage and step around us, he has to pay the price, right? Are we wrong here?*

I better be sure of what I am doing. I can't take back a piano wire twisted around his neck. Maybe I better just shoot him—just wait and ambush him in his car, the revolver will be quick, and out here no one will ever hear it. Even if they do, who cares?

I have learned it is best to let your target decide how they want you to kill them; it's their dance with death. We should at least oblige their final request. My grandmother always taught me it is best to send someone to visit the underworld with happy thoughts. God bless my grandmother and her ancient Alaskan wisdom.

If I was in a job interview right now and someone asked me where I saw myself in five years, honestly I would have to claim to be blind because my horizon has been darkened that much. “I see no future” would be my response. Bleak and barren at best.

The look of terror on a target’s face is the exact reason why I love this part of my job the most, a person’s final look during that exact moment when the realization sets in that they are about to die, and my face is the last thing that they are going to see on this planet.

This is my excitement, my career fulfillment, and it is filled with primal exhilaration. Sort of like the first sunrise cresting the shimmering horizon after a long cold arctic winter up in the interior of Alaska. It gives you a deep sense of knowing everything will be all right.

Tommy was supposed to be alone. It forced me to run in on the passenger’s side of the car to shoot his girlfriend first. I like to remove the witness first because they are more likely to go to the police if they get away. The actual target of the hit is usually not so inclined.

Now he is scrambling to get out of his car and run. Just abandon the love of your life while she bleeds from two in the head; no remorse, no feelings of affection, just run to save yourself. That a boy, Tommy, my man, run, Tommy, run.

I got this scumbag watch this. “Hey, Tommy, do you remember me, man?”

Tommy’s eyes widen, and his mouth is partially open, but no words come out. He is shaking his head back and forth no, no, no.

I slam the barrel of the .357 revolver into his trachea. "I have a message from Maestro. Jethro can't make it tonight. You're fired."

Bang! . . . Bang!

Sweet bacon, did you see that? Holy mackerel, his brains exploded against the door of his car. The second shot hit his heart. Did you see that rusty-colored blood spurting out of the hole? Or is that the smoke that is pouring from out of the hole? Maybe it's both?

Chapter 11

Mystery Infernos Illuminate No Man's Land

Fort Richardson—Arctic Valley, Anchorage, Alaska.

During my first briefing on Fort Richardson about the possible transient camp and the mystery fires of No Man's Land, I am captivated by the intelligence that is being trickled down to us.

This one particular patrol that I was not involved with had just returned to base from the mountains surrounding us. I reported to the Debrief Chambers at 0600 hours as ordered by my squad leader Sergeant Bell. The patrol is trickling in for the meeting as I find my assigned seat along the back wall.

I read the following information written across a big blackboard on the wall:

(1) The fires always get ignited between 2130 and 2200 hours. (2) Approaching 2400 hours the fires are built up into blazing infernos that threaten to ignite the

surrounding forest. (3) The fires are allowed to die back, and by 0400 hours the fires have extinguished themselves.

Sergeant Sidio calls the briefing to order, "Gentlemen, we have a lot to go over. Find a seat." People who are not assigned seating must stand along the back wall.

Sergeant Sidio speaks up, "The hermit of Arctic Valley is at it again. We have a beauty of a report for you all this morning, so strap in for a good time."

Sidio starts laughing. "You will not believe this. We may have found bigfoot in Alaska."

Sidio explains, "As is standard, only initials will be used to identify our team members. No notes will be written. No pictures will be taken. Is that understood?"

Everyone yells, "Yes, Sergeant."

Sidio retorts, "Outstanding. Now let's rock, gentlemen. Team members of 2nd Platoon, 56th Engineers, we are second to none, we're the best now, forget the rest."

Jubilant at the news, everyone in the room screams, "Oorah, oorah, oorah!"

Sidio continues to egg us on, "I can't hear you, 2nd Platoon."

We shout louder, "Oorah, the 2nd Platoon is second to none, we're the best now, forget the rest, Sergeant."

Sergeant Sidio has a maniacal grin plastered across his face as he continues, "I was killing in Vietnam when I was seventeen years old, and I have never heard of anything like this."

"Over the last four nights, Sergeant C. and Specialist T. reported observing more of our mystery fires along the District Utility Plant's powerline trail. Last night they waited, and as 2400 hours approached, the fire was built up into a blazing inferno."

"As the flames grew, they could hear a woman pleading and screaming: 'Why are you doing this to me? Why are you doing this? Don't kill me. Don't kill me.'

"Both Sergeant C. and Specialist T. had weapons configured with infrared night-vision optics. Viewing through their infrared night-vision optics, they observed a white male ritualistically dancing naked around the fire with nothing but his boots and glasses on. They could also hear him howling like a wolf while he gyrated around the fire. Both Sergeant C. and Specialist T. reported nobody else was observed to have been present in the camp."

End of debriefing on Fort Richardson, Alaska.

With our eyes to the horizon, we keep hearing about being the canary in the coal mine guarding the United States against an invasion through Alaska, but we just sit up here on the mountainside staring off to the west. I am getting sick of looking down at this District Utility Plant and the powerline trail. Our only excitement is watching the bonfires from the transient camp that seems to be situated in the treeline below us.

Our chain of command keeps telling us it is just a bunch of crazy drunken transients having a good time out on the edge of the wilderness. Stand down and leave them alone.

Lately, things are getting strange down there. We have been hearing women screaming long hours into the night like bloody murder is upon them. One of the guys tried to make a joke about a premier Alaskan honeymoon destination right here in Arctic Valley for dysfunctional couples. Nobody laughed.

This is our fifth morning out in the mountains during this patrol, and we are watching a lone man below us leave the camp area. It is about 0445 hours, and he is pulling a lawn wagon with balloon tires on it behind him. He also has a rifle slung over his left shoulder.

At first, we pass it off as a moose hunter who may have spent the night out over his kill, but then we realize his wagon is empty, and we see no sign of the woman we had heard screeching her long harsh, piercing cries into the twilight of the night before.

We look back toward the camp, watching a lazy spiral of smoke rising from the dying embers of the fire pit filter up through Sitka Spruce boughs, diffusing and wafting into the heavens above us like silent prayers.

Chapter 12

Maestro Takes Stiletto to Visit Dirk's Bakery

It is with a dispirited relief that I find myself in downtown Anchorage hanging around Snoopy's T-Shirt Shop with Rat and Maestro. Maestro is in the middle of one of his frightening verbal tirades. Unfortunately for me, I am his target this morning.

Maestro has a way of making any person feel pathetically inadequate or unfashionable.

"Stiletto, when are you going to learn to dress? They let you walk off Fort Richardson looking like that, kid? Did the People Mover driver ask you for an ID before he let you board his bus? What is it with you two guys? You both look like crumbled up rags. It's embarrassing for me."

Maestro verbally jumps on Rat and me. He is both forceful and passionate at the same time. "You both need to clean it up out here. Now that's an order, understood? Do you two understand me?"

Both of us are frantically nodding our heads up and down. With urgency both of us sheepishly reply in unison, "Yes, Maestro."

Maestro spits his retort, "Enough said on that then. Next item of contention with you two boneheads. I have arrived here numerous times lately to find the doors locked, and my store is empty. I find you two sitting in the office out back smoking ganja and singing Kumbaya. Are you two for real? Are you two playing me for a monkey out here?"

Rat and I exchange a hurried but worried frown. I am struggling to maintain my resolve. Rat looks ashen faced. My heart is pounding in my ears like a bass drum.

Maestro continues to single me out, pushing me deeper into my mental despair. "Stiletto, I would have expected more from you. You need to maintain the discipline in here for me, or we are going to have chaos. Can you keep the boys off the peace pipe, or is that asking too much? Let's go talk. Now follow me to the office and keep your mouth shut."

Maestro storms toward the office in the back of the store while winding his way through an assortment of overloaded clothes racks with me right on his heels.

Would any of my friends believe this story if I told them? How did I go from being a raw army recruit to mob associate? Is this even considered to be serving my country? Am I living in a parallel universe? This is bizarre, Stiletto man, seriously outrageous.

"Stiletto, shut the door and sit down. Take the box and roll us a joint to smoke. I need to get high while I explain something to you."

As usual, Maestro watches me roll the joint with laser-like vision. His piercing eyes always seem to blaze holes right through me. My steady hands are a must during the rolling.

"I am going to jump right into this, Stiletto. I am getting a piece of business over near midtown. It is a slimy little business that I want no part of at all. This owner has no right to be in business. Now we need to take a ride for a face-to-face with him."

A sharp knock rattles the office door. Maestro abruptly gestures for me to be quiet with his finger to his lips. "Who is it?" he shouts.

"It's Dragonfly, Maestro man. Are we good?"

Maestro motions for me to open the door. Dragonfly walks in, grinning as usual. "Hey, Stiletto man, what's happening, Little Monkey?"

I shrug at him, and Maestro yells, "Why are you asking him what's happening, Dragonfly?"

"Don't I exist anymore? Or am I just invisible now? This is unbelievable—disrespected right in my own office by two hooligans. What are we recasting for the three stooges remake in here?"

"We have big brother Rat, the Little Monkey Stiletto, with the clueless middle twit fluttering around somewhere right in between them like a lost Dragonfly."

Maestro is on a roll. Even the high test marijuana we are smoking doesn't seem to slow him down at all today. This causes Dragonfly and me to melt into a thoughtless dream. It's an easy escape plan.

Maestro knocks on Dragonfly's head with his fist. "You stay here with Rat. Stiletto is taking the ride with me over to Ninth Avenue. Did you put gas in the tank? Please say yes, Dragonfly."

Dragonfly responds, "Maestro man, you know I did. Come on, lay off and be chilled."

Maestro angrily retorts, "I'll be chilled when I die. Do I look dead to you? Do I?"

The ride is quick from 417 D St to 9th Avenue and Ingra St, Dirk's Bakery. It's a nice corner location, with a small side driveway that gives good access to the back door.

In my mind I am trying to imagine what it means to get a piece of a business. With great hesitation I decide to ask Maestro. Maestro seems incensed at my inquiry. "What does it mean to get a piece of business?"

"I am going to show you what it means. That's what it means, Stiletto. You are about to learn one of life's greatest lessons today. Step up and take what's rightfully yours. Now watch and learn from the maestro himself."

As we are backing up into the side driveway, I can see the back door has been left slightly ajar. There is a cracked cinder block being used to prop it open. Maestro shuts the engine down and turns to me. "Stiletto, keep your mouth shut, keep your eyes open, and just watch how I do this in here."

As we step through the back door, I immediately recognize the guy we came to meet.

Hey, this is the same guy that Keith and I threw out of the Wild Cherry last year. We have also detained this guy up on Arctic Valley Road numerous times when Fort

Richardson has gone on full-alert status. I almost didn't recognize him without his rifle, hat, and binoculars on.

When the base goes on full alert, we have to detain and inform the public about the live-fire training exercises that we are about to engage in. We then kindly ask them to leave for their safety. He has been seen in and around No Man's Land on numerous occasions now. We usually bump into him right about 0400 hours at the landing, loading his truck to leave.

Maestro abruptly grabs the owner by the collar and slams him against the wall. He slaps him across his face twice, knocking the man's glasses off him. Then he throws him to the greasy floor like a rag doll.

The owner of Dirk's Bakery looks wild eyed and disheveled, while I take a grateful swallow that it's him on the floor today and not me. His hands have instinctively gone up to protect himself from Maestro's abusive onslaught, and he is vigorously nodding his head back and forth to agree.

Advancing with aggression, Maestro steps over Dirk's quivering body and looks down. "If you ever mess with me, I will bury your whole family, you little worm." Overwrought with fear, Dirks keeps nodding.

Maestro continues, "Look at this guy that is with me, Dirks. See his face?"

Maestro finishes with a scolding rebuke, "Don't you make me send him back here. Don't you ever make me send him back in here. Do you understand me?"

We drive back to Snoopy's in silence along a park that was once an airstrip for landing small airplanes. Many people have come to Alaska for that reason alone—the abundance of pilots and an opportunity to fly among vast mountain ranges seeking the wilderness adventure of a lifetime.

I can't help wondering how many people fly out from Merrill Field and never set eyes on Anchorage again, lost in a harsh wilderness, wandering all alone until they die, or how many planes have gone missing that nobody ever finds.

I also have to wonder maybe some people get flown out for other reasons that are gloomy and more dreadful by design.

Chapter 13

The Trudge into the Devil's Den

Most of the unlucky people who get the invitation to Maestro's house only get it once, and one time only. This is fortunate for them.

Unfortunately for me, this will be my fifth time going to visit the man himself. I am going deep into the lair of the devil's den today, to be pursued by his cold, piercing, steel-blue eyes as they observe every move that I make.

He hugs you and sniffs like a hound dog around your neck while muttering under his breath, "What's that smell on you. Am I smelling panic in here?"

I always meet Rat down at Snoopy's T-Shirt Shop, and he drives me over to Maestro's home somewhere in the city. I really can't figure out where Maestro lives because of the routine we go through every time I visit.

Rat is stoned and smiling as usual when I arrive at 417 D St, and he confirms this with his greeting, "Stiletto, my friend, I am stoned again, my man!"

My response is directed toward the machine we are about to crawl into and drive around Anchorage in. "Who did you guys steal this beast from?"

Rat roars a wild laugh in my direction while retorting, "It was a gift for Maestro from an extremely loving fan, and we get to test drive it for him, my friend. Now put the blindfold on and strap in tight, my man."

I tie the blindfold around my entire head as they instructed me to do. We do a full wrap around my face with a tight back knot. There is a slit cut for a mouth port.

We are driving in a cherry red 1967 Chevy Camaro, which is all I know, and we are driving very fast around Anchorage. Rat breaks every speed limit on all the streets we drive on. After twenty minutes of his white knuckle maneuvers, the car lurches to a stop, and Rat yells, "Quick, take off the blindfold."

We are sitting in front of Snoopy's T-Shirt Shop again, still disorientated from the furious roller-coaster ride we have just been through. Rat yells, "Blindfold up."

I obey, and we repeat this process three times over the next hour or so. Slamming his brakes on, backing up, and turning around is all involved to add to my disorientation.

Finally, we arrive at a familiar spot. We always park at the same trailhead in the same cul-de-sac, and we walk from here. I am instructed not to look at any street signs while we walk and to keep my head down. We remove the blindfold to avoid any curious eyes.

We walk in silence while I follow Rat along a grassy embankment. Maestro has no number on his house. He picks all of his mail and packages up at the post office, so he doesn't have to have anyone unexpected on his property for any reason.

I know we are by the water because I can smell the salt hanging in the air, and the sky is filled by a flock of gulls singing—they're echoing forlorn cries. *Should I try to sneak a peek? If Rat notices, I am done here. Don't do it, Stiletto. Don't sneak a peek, man. Am I insane; really am I insane?*

We arrive at the grayish-blue house with white trim after walking for about twenty minutes in silence, when Rat suddenly speaks up, "Stiletto, Maestro is on edge this morning. Do not infuriate him again with our tales of unheard feelings, man."

"Maestro disagrees with all of this talk about how we feel left out of things. The talk he has been hearing coming from the store lately is upsetting him. He is looking for some recognition from his crew. Now let's go pay the boss some homage."

We get buzzed into the inside foyer. There is a camera that is pointing at a second door, and Rat has to ring a second doorbell before we enter.

This is the part of these visits I hate the most. As we get buzzed through the second door, we immediately start climbing a fairly steep staircase, and standing sentinel at the top of the stairs are two very burly guys dressed in suits.

Here we go again. Maestro's gorilla gang is on duty—great, I am about to be slammed against a wall. *How did I get myself into this mess? Is this worth fifty cents an hour? Be all that you can be? Is this all I can be? Getting slapped around and threatened by thugs? I want my recognition. Where's my recognition?*

"Lift your arms, Stiletto." I lift my arms while the two bodyguards pat and shake me down. "He's clear. No weapons," they yell over toward Maestro.

Here it comes. They both smirk at me.

One of the bodyguards grabs me and slams me against the wall face first. He pushes his forearm against the back of my neck and inches in closely to my left ear. "If you even look at Maestro the wrong way, you are dead. When you get within three feet of him, your hands better be behind your back, or you're dead. Are we good, Stiletto?"

He spins me around and pushes me over toward Maestro's wide open arms. Maestro is smiling, saying, "Stiletto, long time no see, Little Monkey. Welcome into my house. Please feel at home while you are here today." Maestro embraces me tightly like a stealthy boa constrictor squeezing her squirming prey.

I respond, "Maestro, thank you for inviting me to visit, sir. I love your home."

"No need to call me sir at this point in our relationship, Little Monkey, but I like your train of thought. I want you to follow me. I have something I want to show you."

Maestro spins and unexpectedly grabs my head with both of his slimy hands. He kisses me on my forehead with wet slobbering lips and whispers into my ear, "If you ever tell anyone what I am about to show you, you're a dead man. If I ever see you uninvited in my neighborhood, you're a dead man, Little Monkey."

I assure him, "Maestro, I have no idea where I am. Are we even still in Alaska? I see nothing, says this blind man. Can I even see you?"

Maestro smiles. "I love you, Stiletto, but you better be seeing me. Can you see this?" as he pushes his clenched fist firmly up against my face.

Maestro leads me over to an amazing granite table that has a black cloth spread out over the top of it. There is a hanging light illuminating the table in a gentle ghostly luminescencc.

I watch as he pulls back the top velvet cloth and reveals a sparkling pile of what looks like melted glass. With two mischievous eyes, Maestro grins. "This is ice, Stiletto, raw uncut diamonds sent to me straight from South Africa."

My body stiffens. This is the first mention of South Africa that CID warned me about.

OK, now it gets deep here. Is this why he always talks about being a monkey? Has Maestro been to South Africa? What is his connection to South Africa? Why Africa?

I can't help myself, and I blurt out, "Maestro, what would these diamonds be worth converted into cash?"

Maestro freezes, his body stiffens, and he growls, "Three-and-a-half million dollars, Stiletto, that's if you use my scales, and it depends on the final cut."

Maestro continues to explain, "Clarity is a concern with this batch," while he reaches for a monocle. "We do not want to detect inclusions, but I want you to notice these little black specks. We shouldn't be seeing these with our naked eyes. This is why cut will become important for the final dollar tally with this batch."

I honestly have no idea what he just explained to me—clarity, cut? Ice? Diamonds?

Next, he reaches under the table and pulls out a fairly hefty leather handbag—it's about the size of a bowling ball bag, and he hoists it up onto the granite tabletop. Maestro looks at me, and again he has a mischievous grin. "Unzip this beautiful Betty for me, Stiletto. I want your eyes to behold this—this is the purest gold in the land, my friend. This is not some scrap metal being pulled from a silty Alaskan stream. This is the finest metal, Little Monkey, given to us by mother earth herself."

Nonchalantly, I grab the bag and unzip it. Inside I see many white plastic tubes that appear to be filled with gold coins. My estimate is easily one hundred tubes.

Maestro can't hold back any longer. He is bursting to speak. "Stiletto, these are one ounce South African gold Krugerrands. Each casing houses twenty coins. You are looking at two thousand Krugerrands, Little Monkey."

Maestro continues, "There's another bag just like it where that one came from. Each bag weighs about seventy two pounds. At today's prices, the four thousand ounces of gold is worth approximately two-and-a-half million dollars."

OK, I am standing next to well over six million dollars. This is becoming a little intimidating for me now. How did I get here in this room? What would make the universe call me down this trail? Is any of this gold for me?

I shake my head in disbelief, and Maestro smiles. "I know it's hard to fathom right now, Stiletto, but if you decide to join me all in, you will be wealthy like this someday."

Maestro wraps his sinewy arm around my shoulders in a fatherly fashion. "Little Monkey, I want you to have a drink with me. I have a very fine cognac from France."

We walk over to a magnificent fireplace where we meet a very beautiful blonde woman. She is standing behind a little bar nook mixing cocktails for her and Rat, and I can hear the gentle tinkling of the ice cubes as she stirs.

Maestro introduces her as his fiancé. She is an amazing woman, strikingly alluring, but he never tells me her name and just calls her his fiancé. They both smile longingly into each other's eyes for several awkward moments, before she asks me what I am drinking.

Her accent, along with her long blond hair, dark-blue eyes, and luscious, long lashes has me mesmerized. I am dancing through a minefield of affections right in front of the boss.

I reply, "Cognac on the rocks."

Maestro spins and screams at me, "On the rocks? No, no on the rocks in my house. This is my house, my rules, no rocks."

He chillingly glares at his fiancé. Normally I would have ignored him, but I am in a hostile mood. "Maestro, it's chill, brother, rocks, no rocks . . . who cares, man?"

A switch flips, and Maestro rants, "Don't come into my house and get between me and my woman, Stiletto.

She knows the rules. Now stand over there in the corner before I slap you in the face."

He is pointing his sharp finger toward a gloomy corner next to a big African battle shield that is hanging on the wall. Feeling rather glum and resigned, I dutifully obey him.

This shield is strange. And what are all these black statues about? Are these all South African artifacts? That's a wicked-looking spear hanging above the fireplace, its jagged-edge spear point blade ready to tear into soft flesh. Is that from Africa also?

South African Krugerrands? Uncut diamonds? Ice? Scolded and punished for wanting ice in my drink?

Chapter 14

Maestro Puts Suspecting Eyes on Dirk's Bakery

"Listen to me, Stiletto. Maestro means you no harm. He only wants what's best for you out here, Little Monkey. Maestro wants you to move up and flex your muscle more for us."

I reply, "Dragonfly man, if I start dressing up, I will look out of place out here, and you know there is nobody on the streets of Anchorage right now worried about how I dress."

Dragonfly squints his eyes in disbelief while retorting, "Maestro cares. He is on me about it. Why wouldn't he be on you about it? Why are you going to make me have to kill you if Maestro snaps? Stay alive. Buy two shirts. JC Penny is close to Snoopy's."

Dejected, maybe even a little dismayed, I just shake my head yes in response.

There are no words to describe the chaotic turmoil that is churning in my stomach. It started as a low rumble and has evolved into a burning volcano deep in the pit of my gut.

If I start playing the game their way, then whose side am I on? Am I being asked to switch uniforms here? Should I be the villain and cooperate? Do I need to see Lieutenant McCrackin on this? Is Lieutenant McCrackin CID? Does CID see all this?

Maestro sent us over to spy on Dirk's Bakery. Now I am sitting in a drab dented orange taxi and listening to a degenerate street killer tell me I need to dress in better clothes.

We are sitting along Ingra St at E Ninth Avenue and watching for Damon Dirks to leave his bakery so we can follow him. Maestro suspects he is dipping his fingers into a forbidden pie. It is how it was explained to me. I have no idea what that even means, but it does not sound good for Dirks.

I was curious recently and started reading about the origination of some of the names being used in Anchorage for street names, parks, and municipal buildings. I read that Ingra loosely interprets to mean a girl with a bullheadish attitude toward life.

We are also sitting close to the intersection with E Ninth Avenue. In the occult, and in the Bible, the number nine is the number of judgment.

Is this a dire warning to any bullheaded girl walking the streets of Anchorage that judgment is right at their doorstep? Is Dirk's Bakery somehow symbolic of this impending doom? Is Damon, the owner of Dirk's Bakery, somehow judge, jury, and executioner of any woman he perceives as bullheaded? What is bullheaded?

Dragonfly's raspy voice draws me out of my daydream. "Stiletto, this is some nasty stuff this little twerp is involved with. A lot of our dancers have been going missing. It's very bad for our business, my man. It's bringing the whole vibe of Fourth Avenue down the drain."

I can't believe how frightened I am getting as the picture starts to become more clear for me. Eyes wide, mouth partially open, I turn to Dragonfly and ask, "Are you telling me this may be the guy who is kidnapping all of the exotic dancers and prostitutes in Anchorage? Dragonfly man, I need to know."

Gravely, Dragonfly responds, "He might not be responsible for all of them, but he is, for most of them. Yes, that's what I am telling you, Little Monkey, my man, he is a depraved imbecile."

"Dragonfly, I need your help with something, man. I had a friend I was hanging around with last year, and she disappeared. Last time I saw her was several days before she was doing a photo shoot for three hundred dollars with a guy she called a little twerp."

Dragonfly keeps looking intently into my eyes; he responds, "What's her name?"

I reply, "Angie Altman. They call her Fish sometimes because of a necklace she wears, and when she dances, her stage name is Enchantment."

He shrugs. "Never heard of her, but if she hasn't danced at one of Maestro's clubs, I wouldn't have had contact with her. Unless she got into my taxi, but I never ask names.

Who cares about people's names up here in Alaska, man?" He continues, "So do you like this girl, Little Monkey?"

I hesitate, "Kind of, yes, OK, maybe a lot of yes. It's her eyes, Fly. It's her eyes, man! I spent two months of heart-churning, burning desire waiting to look into them again."

"Well, what happened? Don't leave me hanging here, man," Dragonfly responds.

Despondently, I sigh, "Look, Fly, we never met up again. She went missing, man."

Dragonfly starts laughing. "Stiletto has a love interest, man. Let's hope she is all right where ever she is. Don't worry, there are plenty of available women in this world, Little Monkey. Trust me, kid, a guy like you—you're a babe for the ladies, Stiletto man."

I appreciate his confidence in my ability to meet women, but honestly, I don't feel the vibe myself. *Who would want to date a man without a country? What woman would choose to be with a guy like me?* There is not a single woman in Anchorage who wants to be with me. All I keep finding is remorseful hate in this town.

Dragonfly nudges me with his sharp, pointy elbow. "There's the dirty devil himself. Strap in and get ready to roll, my friend."

Dirks just walked out of the back door of his bakery and is throwing a few items into the back of an older beat-up-looking station wagon, probably his wife's car, by the looks of it.

We casually follow Damon Dirks as he drives north on Ingra St up to where it merges onto E Sixth Avenue for a short stretch before merging again into E Fifth Ave and the Glenn Highway. We all get off at the Muldoon Rd exit about four miles up the highway. Our drive is silently melancholic.

Dirk pulls into the parking lot of a notoriously dingy confine named Sportsman II, a lower-end exotic dance club known more for their novice dancers. It profits from being very close to two mid-size military bases located nearby on the outskirts of Anchorage.

We drive by and continue for about a mile along Muldoon Rd before Dragonfly turns us around in a Tesoro gas station parking lot. We circle back to the Sportsman II and pull into the parking lot.

Dragonfly immediately sets eyes on Dirks' vehicle and pulls us to the furthest point we can get away from him, while still being able to see his car. We can see a shadow silhouetted in the driver's seat. Dragonfly motions for me to crouch down low in my seat. He puts his finger to his lips and gives me a big "Shoosh."

I shrug and squint my eyes. "Don't shoosh me!"

He retorts, "Stiletto!"

With due notice I get the message. Our silence is golden right now.

I mean I know it's his car, but Dirks is about one hundred yards away from us. Is he for real? Shoosh? Shoosh! Did he just shoosh me? Don't shoosh me! No matter where I find myself, everyone else seems to be setting my agenda. Is this my destiny? No say in the matter ever? Just shoosh? Shoosh?

We sit and wait for about forty-five minutes, when we notice a shadowy figure coming from the back of the Sportsman II approaching Dirks' vehicle. We watch him step on his brakes three times to signal the person. The red flashing is reflecting off a nearby car.

This reminds me of a song that I used to listen to: "Red flashes in the sky, / warn you that you are about to die." *I think it was a Black Sabbath song.*

The person pulls their hood back just before reaching for the handle of Dirks' car. Her long, flowing blond hair spills out into the gentleness of the night breeze.

I just can't help it. The song keeps pounding through my head as I watch: "Red flashes in the sky, / warn you that you are about to die." Tonight someone is going for a death ride. Filled with gripping terror, I turn to Dragonfly, pleading with him in agony.

Shaking my head, I am saying, "We need to help her, man. We can't let him kill her, dude. Come on, let's get him. Let's go!"

The Fly growls, "Stand down, Little Monkey. It's not our call. If we make a move, Maestro will bury both of us. Now, shoosh!"

Shoosh again? Did this guy just hit me with another shoosh? This guy is irreverent.

Another song starts playing in my mind: "Somewhere out there in this world we are all wanted either dead or alive, / it just depends on who comes knocking at your front door.

Chapter 15

Damon Dirks: The Owner

I am sitting in the back office at Snoopy's T-Shirt Shop, smoking a joint of very fine marijuana with Rat. We are both waiting for Maestro and Dragonfly to arrive at the store.

Rat has spent the last fifteen minutes explaining to me that Maestro has a mission for me—his words, not mine. Now I am curious, to say the least. A mission sounds formal. It has a tone of urgency that stirs something deep within me.

Finally, Maestro storms the office with Dragonfly right on his heels. The first thing he does is bark out an order. "Rat, get lost. I don't want to see your ugly face."

I can feel the evil radiating off both these men. They both seethe. Their mouths seem to foam with anger like a pack of mad dogs found howling in the cold, windy streets. With some ferocity, they suddenly turn their attention on me.

Maestro rants, "Stiletto, if you ever tell anyone what we are about to ask you to do for us, I will personally kill you, understood?" not waiting for my answer, he continues, "If I can't kill you, I know Dragonfly can. Is that understood?"

Again not waiting for any type of answer, Maestro goes on, "We need you to send a message to that friend of ours over in midtown. Now I know you have been over there with both myself and Dragonfly, so there is no need to say the name of the business, understood?"

This time he waits for my reply. I am rudely brief. "Yes, Maestro, understood."

Maestro goes silent. Solemnly he looks between Dragonfly and me. "Do you boys understand what I am offering you two? We are talking real wealth, guys, real cash. Remember, cash is always going to be king in this world."

We allow the boss to continue without interruption and go on he does. "Stiletto, I am sending you in as an applicant. You told me a story about working in a bakery during high school—is that true?"

I respond, "Yes, I worked as a baker's aide, not a head baker. It is a nice Portuguese bakery right in the center of my home town. They make great donuts."

Maestro replies, "That's OK. That's going to be good enough. Just walk in casually someday and inquire, grab an application for me, and get it filled out. Now listen to me, Stiletto, you need to make the owner believe that if he makes any more mistakes then you, and I mean you, are going to send Dragonfly."

I speak up and ask, "Maestro, what's the message I am sending?"

"Two messages—first that you are the only person authorized to give Dragonfly orders other than myself, and the second message is this, Little Monkey. Tell him Maestro needs you to keep the salmon running twenty-four hours a day for the next six months. Can you remember that?"

I respond, "Yes, Maestro needs you to keep the salmon running twenty-four hours a day for the next six months."

Maestro inquires, "And what's the second message, Stiletto?"

Quickly I reply, "I have been authorized by Maestro to use Dragonfly's name and give him orders at Maestro's request."

Maestro smiles. "I love you, Little Monkey. Just don't make us have to kill you. It would be a real shame to lose you, kid."

I know I am crazy for staying in this and not going to Lieutenant McCrackin, but I know CID has had their eyes on me. They could have pulled me out at any time. *Have they turned their backs on me? Am I alone without any hope? Is life hopeless for most of us? What is hope?* I would like to find out someday soon.

I cross the street and am walking up a little hill along a small embankment as the smell is getting stronger. I know I am now close to the source of the smell. I come up along a cinder block building that has Dirk's Bakery occupying the corner. As I get to the storefront, I can read Dirk's Bakery stenciled on the window in bold lettering.

They are offering baked goods fresh daily, along with donuts and cookies. I also see a "Help Wanted" sign on the window as I am walking in. Two women are working behind the counter—both look over at me as the bell on the door starts ringing.

I am glad to be out of the cold and wind. I ask the woman who approaches me if they sell pizza, and she kindly laughs at me. OK, no pizza but they do have donuts, so I order two plain donuts to go. As the first woman gets the donuts, the second lady comes over and asks me if there will be anything else for me today.

I tell her, "Yes, I saw your 'Help Wanted' sign, and I am looking for a part-time evening job. I would like to fill out an application, and I will buy a carton of milk also." She gets both items for me and places them up on the counter.

Both women tell me that the owner of the bakery is away for a few more days on a personal trip, and they also tell me to come back in about three to five days and speak with him.

I ask them if I can take the application with me so it is already completed when I return, and they say yes. OK, nice, I have donuts, milk, and a job application. I leave knowing I will be back to confront Dirks for Maestro; menacing tones need be applied.

During the week I get the application filled out for the bakery and plan my trip downtown for this coming Saturday. In my experience, Saturday is an all-hands-on-deck for a bakery crew. I am thinking Dirks will be there after being away from the business for a while.

Saturday morning I decide not to eat over at our chow hall on base. Instead, I decide to call a taxi and go to get breakfast at the Lucky Wishbone restaurant on E Fifth Ave. After that, I will walk straight down Karluk St to E Ninth Avenue to get over to Dirk's Bakery and drop off this application.

The waitress can't believe I don't want coffee. I tell her I would prefer a milkshake this morning, chocolate if possible. I go with a simple breakfast today: two scrambled eggs, rye toast with a side of bacon, and the world's best chocolate malt milkshake.

I grab a newspaper from the table next to me and start reading an in-depth story about all the exotic dancers and prostitutes who have been going missing for the last year or so now. This was the big news story when I first landed in Alaska—Eklutna Annie and Joanne Messina had been all over the news back then.

When the waitress returns to my table, she sees the story that I am reading and says, "That's a scary and sad situation, you know." I console her, then tell her it's a nasty situation Anchorage is dealing with right now. Let us hope they catch this guy as soon as possible.

She agrees with me, then changes the subject. "Hey, it's going to be a nice day out there today, right. Let's both be happy." I smile back at her while thinking, *I am about to stand face-to-face with this monster. He is known as Damon Dirks.*

I can see his bakery is busy from where I am standing on Ninth Avenue. I cross Ingra Street over into the parking lot while thinking, *Hope Dirks is in and can find time to speak with me this morning. I don't want to come back here if I can avoid it. I don't like this guy at all, and I'm sure he doesn't like me either.*

I hold the door open for an older gentleman exiting the bakery and then two ladies entering the store before I step inside.

The counter and register area are very crowded with eager customers waiting in line. Amazing smells thickly swirl around us with subtle seduction. I see the woman who gave me the job application, and I try to get her attention. She looks over at me and holds one finger up, signaling for me to wait my turn while she rings up her customer.

When she completes her transaction, the lady waves me over to her while wiping her hands on her apron. "I remember you, smiley," she says.

I hand her the application, saying, "I told you I would come back. I just couldn't resist your smile. Is the owner here today?"

With a brimming smile, the lady replies, "Smiley, you are in luck. Except for his two-hour break to run home and check on things, he has been working all night. I am sure he will want to speak with you." She asks for me to wait while she brings my application out back to him so that he can quickly review it.

When she comes back out to the front, she informs me it will be about twenty minutes before he will be able to speak with me. "If that's too long of a wait, I understand, sugar," she says with a huge grin.

"No problem, ma'am, I can wait for him outside."

I finally see Damon Dirks coming out from the back production area. He pushes through the door while reading my application. He slowly walks over to the lady whom I had spoken with, and as they talk with each other, she points through the window toward me.

He looks at me with his head tilted. He is pushing up the bridge of his glasses. He looks down at my application again, then shakes his head. When I realize he is coming outside to speak with me, I start walking toward the door to greet him.

As Dirks steps through the bakery door, I extend my hand out to shake his hand, but he walks right past me and quickly segregates me away from the front entry area off to the right side of the storefront.

Sullenly staring up at me, his squeaky voice asks, "Why are you here? What is this all about, Little Monkey? Am I in trouble with Maestro?"

He recognizes me for sure, and he is frightened. Slightly sputtering, he continues, "I . . . I mean . . . I always want to help you guys in any way I can. How can I help you guys? Just tell me what I need to do to help you all out over there. I keep telling Maestro this, Little Monkey, please."

I reply, "Dirks man, I don't like your donuts. That's the first order of business. Second, I am the only person authorized to give Dragonfly orders other than Maestro himself. Third, Maestro needs you to keep your head in the game twenty-four hours a day for the next six months. Listen to me, Dirks, if you don't keep your head in the game, I will have to send Dragonfly back here. Is that understood? Do you understand me?"

He looks exhausted. Emphatically he silently nods his head yes; then he gives me a half wave over his shoulder as he skulks away to the inside of his bakery. Never once does he look back toward me.

Was I just talking with the monster of Fourth Avenue? Is this guy capable of the horrendous crimes being committed against women in Anchorage? What would make a person want to intentionally and deliberately kill another human being just for fun? Do they just want to amuse themselves with other people's pain and suffering?

Chapter 16

Summoned into the Devil's Den Once Again

Here I find myself about to stroll into the stem of the devil's den once again for the sixth time. It's only a matter of time before I don't come out alive.

This must be a different kind of meeting with Maestro today. When I walked into Snoopy's this morning to meet Rat, he pulled a rusty machete out from under the front counter and did a two-minute kung fu kata around my head while issuing dire warnings and threatening me with decapitation.

He finished by pushing the point of the blade up under the bottom of my chin, causing a small freckle of blood splotch to appear with this dire threat: "If you ever tell anyone what we are about to talk with you about, you are dead, Stiletto."

Then we drove directly to the cul-de-sac where Maestro lives without my blindfold on and no dizzying drive across the city. *Are they bringing me in on a whole different level? What's going on here? Am I walking into a trap? Are they going to kill me today? Is this it for me?*

Once we enter through the second door leading out of the foyer, I notice with a quiet surprise that Maestro does not have his two burly bodyguards working this morning. No looks of rebuke come my way as I ascend the steep stairs of Satan.

When I get to the top of the stairs, I see Maestro sweeping across the living room in a graceful dance. It looks like he is doing the tango with an inspiring but invisible partner of elegance.

The cuffs of his crisply pressed white dress shirt are neatly rolled back, exposing his hairy forearms, one is laden with a gem-encrusted gold watch. A precise instrument for sure.

Maestro twirls toward me and motions for me to join the dance with him. Feeling uneasy and very embarrassed, I decide to oblige my boss. Maestro leads me into a twirl. He is graceful with his lead and pushes me into a spin.

Suddenly becoming enraged with fury, Maestro grabs me and runs my body into a nearby wall—the collision has me seeing stars. Maestro is growling into my ear, "Little Monkey, if you ever tell anyone about today, you're a dead man."

I am looking into the frozen, wild eyes of a stone-cold killer. He radiates evil with his every snorting breath. His temper burns through every muscle in his taut body.

I reach my hand out to him and receive a wet, limp shake.

Rat is quietly sitting on one of the couches in another room. Maestro motions for me to follow him while he explains, "Stiletto, my business is being hurt by whoever it is that is kidnapping these dancers out there. We think we now know for sure who it is. The prostitutes do not affect me, but the girls that want to dance are afraid. Some are leaving Alaska for the lower forty-eight. I can't have this anymore. Finding quality women in Alaska is tough enough. Competing with a deranged killer takes us to another playing field. We need to eliminate this competition, Stiletto."

There comes a point in most conversations when heads start to shake. With Maestro, your body starts to quake. Most people change names to protect the innocent. Maestro changes names to protect the not-so innocent. Maestro motions for me to sit with him. He leans in close. "Stiletto, I have an opportunity for you, kid. I need a director of security, and I want you to have that position."

Maestro is beaming as he continues, "You already know about my annual Hawaii to Homer operation. We have a huge harvest coming to us this year, Stiletto, huge, my friend. I am going to need someone like you on the mother boat as we load the product. Once we start loading, it will take us three days to complete."

Curiously, Maestro hesitates, so I speak up, "What's the compensation?"

Maestro shakes his head smiling. "I love you, my man, always right to the point."

He lays it all out for me like a CEO expounding on his corporate vision showcasing his company's bright future, with me acting as one of his rising stars.

"Little Monkey, I will give you a team of five guys. You can have the weapons of your choice. I prefer small arms, but ultimately that will be your decision."

I respond, "For the team, I want Russian AKMs. Each man will be locked and loaded, carrying three hundred rounds in reserve. For me, I want a Mossberg 500 twelve-gauge shotgun and an M60 machine gun. No handguns will be allowed."

Maestro comes over and embraces me. "We can do this. We can do this together."

He continues, "The compensation is this in a nutshell, Stiletto. Three weeks in Hawaii, all your expenses paid, and thirty thousand dollars cash will be paid per week. About five weeks after the job is complete, you will receive seven pounds of top-notch marijuana to do with as you wish. As head of my security, the rest of the year you will work as a doorman at my after-hours clubs being paid six hundred dollars cash per week under the table, and all your drinks and women are free. You will live rent-free in my six-plex over near Fifteenth Avenue and Eagle St. Including the rent, that's a street value of $153,400 annually. How's that for a compensation plan, Little Monkey?"

Chapter 17

Dirty Dirks at Denali

It's 6:35 p.m. when I finally get my table. I prefer not eating in a bar area, so the wait was well worth it for me. I order snow crab legs with a frozen white Russian. With a seductive smile, my waitress tells me my order is sexy. "Your order is sexy. I'll be right back with hot steamy rolls just for you," she replies.

Is she flirting with me? Why would she flirt with me? Maybe she is? How can a food order be sexy? Women always get me confused.

The meal is unusually great tonight. When I ask my waitress for the check, she introduces herself to me. "Hi, my name's Katherine. Would you mind if I sit down for a minute to speak with you about something?"

"Speak to me? Sure, sit down, Katherine, please. My name is Little Monkey," I reply.

Katherine doesn't hesitate. "Do you need to get slapped tonight, honey?" At first, I am not sure what she means.

Embarrassed, and feeling a little bewildered, it suddenly hits me what she is asking me to do.

Smiling, I lean in a little closer across the table toward her. She continues to seduce me. "You need a good slap tonight, don't ya, Little Monkey?" Laughing, but keeping the thought to myself, *I understand this is the definition of an Alaskan happy meal at Club Paris.*

When I finally get outside, it feels good to start walking again. I decide to walk the entire length of Fourth Avenue one more time from L St up to Juneau St. Let's see whom I randomly bump into out here.

A stiff, cold wind pushes me along for a while before I enter a rowdy area where the Wild Cherry and the Booby Trap exotic dance clubs are. As I am approaching the intersection of E Fourth Avenue with Cordova St, my eyes fall on ten to fifteen girls gathered on the other side of the street in a large group.

I think I recognize one of the girls, so I cross the street to see if it's her. Two or three of the girls turn and look my way. They all start yelling at once. "It's the Little Monkey. It's the Little Monkey." Frantically all the girls start talking.

"Little Monkey, help us. A weird, scary guy is offering us three hundred dollars to do photo shoots. He won't leave us alone. He slowly drives by us; then he goes down and pulls onto Denali St and parks for a while, waiting to see if one of us will run down to him. Please help us get rid of him. Make him leave us alone."

"Girls, please, one at a time. What are you saying about three hundred dollars?" I ask.

One of the girls pushes forward to speak with me. "Little Monkey, he pulls up in his pickup truck camper and asks if one of us would like to go with him and do a photo shoot for three hundred dollars. 'It'll be quick, fun, and easy," he keeps saying.'"

Another one of the girls explains to me, "Every one of us keeps telling him to get lost, but he has been circling us for almost an hour now. At least an hour, I would say." All the other girls are anxiously nodding.

I've been hearing this nonsense about a $300 photo shoot for almost two years now, and I'm getting sick of it. Angie told me the guy who offered her $300 to do a photo shoot was kind of weird, but she thought he was harmless. She assured me she could take anybody in a fight. I haven't seen her since.

I shout out to the girls, "Let's go, let's all go down there, and we will confront him about this together." Five or six of the girls start to follow me as I briskly walk down E Fourth Avenue toward Denali St. "Let's go see who this guy is," I keep repeating this to the girls while we walk a hundred yards to Denali St.

If this is Dirks, he is getting done tonight. I don't need the Maestro's or CID's permission to pound this puke out here. Do I? Do I need to stand down if it's Dirks? This can't be Dirks.

I have a nice pair of black leather gloves on, and it's cold out here. The leather will rip skin like a surgical razor blade. As we turn the corner onto Denali St, I can see an older pickup truck with a camper top that I recognize immediately. I have seen this truck up in Arctic Valley, and I have seen this truck over at Dirk's Bakery—it's Dirks; it's him.

Dirty Dirks must have seen us because his brake lights have come on. I yell for the girls to quickly start making snowballs. With pumping adrenaline we start throwing them at the back of his truck. When Dirks shifts his truck into gear, the tires start spinning, sending his truck sliding sideways into the unforgiving curb with a crunch.

I get the chance I need to run up alongside his truck. Shouting obscenities, I start banging wildly on his camper until I get to the driver's side door. His tires are buzzing strangely on the ice. I can smell the rubber from his burning tires. Dirks looks directly into my eyes. He has a horrified look on his face. I start knocking on his driver's window. He seems to recognize me.

I start screaming at him. "Stop the vehicle, Dirks. You're done, Dirks. Get out. You're done. Stop this vehicle, Dirks." Damon Dirks has a look of sheer terror on his face that will be ingrained in my mind forever.

Suddenly his tires grab onto some dry pavement, the truck lurches forward, and he gets about fifty feet up Denali St before he starts to slow down again. One of the girls and I keep running after him with frozen balls of dripping snow in our hands.

The girl who is with me is dressed in a way I will never be able to forget—she's wearing high heels with pink fishnet stockings, a red leather skirt, a blue leather jacket that has long tassels, a white cowboy hat covering her thick blond hair.

We both continue to throw snowballs at the back of Dirks' truck while he slowly drives off, trailed by an eerie sounding exhaust, a chillingly creaky suspension that keeps echoing down Denali St, reverberating back to us up that spooky road.

With exuberance, the woman turns and high-fives me. "Wow, that was intense, Little Monkey. Thank you." We slap hands. The rest of the girls have now made it around the corner, and I tell them all, "Be careful out there. Be wary. Stay vigilant."

All of a sudden I hear a car horn blaring and beeping. A taxi has pulled over for me, and my good friend Keith Bryan from Fort Richardson is shouting for me to get in. "Stiletto, let's go, man. Hurry up. Get in."

The taxi driver is a woman, and she is talking to us about lost loves. "I've been divorced four times," she explains. Then she tries to drag us into the drama of her last divorce. I drown her voice out in my mind by thinking about Damon Dirks on Denali St.

It terrifying and haunting knowing I can't stop this guy. There's much in this life we can't comprehend. Strange, eerie. I can't think straight . . . can't see clearly. Scary, unsettling to think, as the song goes "Lock up your daughters, / lock up your wives."

Chapter 18

De Luciano: CID Burns the Specialist

The cabin heater for the personnel carrier we are riding in is working great this morning as we bounce back up to the ski lodge along Arctic Valley Road. Our physical training for today is Nordic skiing and traversing the five-mile mountain trail that runs from the small bridge at the broken-down fence just below the lodge.

We have already had three great runs this morning. All of us are skiing on Rossignol 280 cm skis. It is ten degrees below zero, and the overall skiing conditions are beyond pristine. It is great for building mutual trust and friendship among a group of guys who spend a lot of time together in harsh environments.

As you come to the end of the ski run approaching Arctic Valley Road, you have to ski up and over a very large snow berm that has been amassed, and left behind over some time by all the busy snowplow trucks navigating the steep inclines and switchbacks of this frozen mountain road.

As I am approaching the berm, my trail partner, Bryone, gives me a big thumbs up for another successful and safe run. We exchange smiles, and he nods me forward to go in front of him over the berm where the trail narrows. I hit the squeeze right on the line and bounce up over the crest of the berm.

The personnel carrier is nowhere to be seen, but I can see three MP jeeps with their lights flashing waiting below me, their idling engines betrayed by the lazy exhaust smoke rising from their rusty tailpipes.

My squad leader, Sergeant Bell, is standing with two military police officers, and they are pointing over at me as I bend down to grab my skis. Sergeant Bell's voice bellows out to me, "De Luciano, we have a problem. You now have a problem, soldier. Right now you need not make any rash judgments here, soldier. Stand down and go peacefully with these MPs back down to the base. Is that understood, De Luciano?"

I curtly retort, "Yes, Sergeant."

Sergeant Bell takes my equipment from me while the five MP officers surround me. One of the MPs removes his service baton and circles around behind me while the other officers all step aside. I just stand tight looking straight ahead, not blinking.

Out of the corner of my eye, I see the MP jump down into a kneeling position, and he thrusts the baton straight through my heavily clothed legs.

He quickly pulls back while twisting the baton so it crosses my shin bones. He grabs me by the back of my collar, viciously slamming me face-first into the frozen ground while screaming, “You are being arrested under the UCMJ. I advise you not to struggle with us today.”

All the of other MPs rush in over my prone body like a pack of proud jackals. I can hear the clinking of chains being drawn against each other while they secure my hands and feet tightly together behind my back.

One of the MPs wraps a chain around my waist, and then they link it all together in one big bundle of chains wrapped around me like an expensive Christmas present. Then they slide their service batons into the chains and use them to hoist me up onto the hood of one of the jeeps, face down.

I am looking down at the local District Utility Plant’s powerline and the trail that runs along with it. We call that No Man’s Land down there. Right now I’m not sure I even have a country to call home anymore.

Once they secure me in the back of the jeep and we start driving, I speak up, “Are you guys CID or 562nd MPs?”

They exchange looks. The driver responds matter of factly, “562nd MPs soldier now stand down back there.”

OK, good, they are not CID; maybe this is just a big mistake being made. Is that wishful thinking? Looking at the past two years. I have to wonder sometimes whose side I am actually on here; have I crossed the line? Is there even a line to cross? Has anybody ever witnessed another person stepping or jumping over an imaginative line? Is that even a real question?

As we pass through the Moose Run Golf course, the corporal sitting in the passenger’s seat casually comments back over his shoulder, "You are looking at twenty-five to life in Leavenworth, soldier. I hope they throw the key away on you."

Both guys start howling like victorious wolves. I can hear the driver bragging, "I thought they briefed us on this guy and told us he was going to be a very difficult arrest. Difficult my aching back."

Once we arrive at building #664 that houses my barracks, we are met by my new commanding officer, Major Kaldenberg, and our executive officer, Lieutenant McCrackin. Both men have serious looks of dejection etched upon their stone-cold faces as they escort me and the three MP officers into the building.

I am still chained, but at least they allow me the dignity of hobbling up the front stairs, pulling myself along a wobbly and rusty railing with broken support collars. We are met by First Sergeant Blankenship. He is an extremely intimidating human being.

Two of the MPs stop and stand guard at the top of the stairs while I am escorted through the hall by Commanding Officer Major Kaldenberg, Executive Officer Lieutenant McCrackin, First Sergeant Blankenship, and one MP officer pulling rear guard for them.

Every soldier we walk by is standing at attention, looking straight ahead like a statue. No one even glances my way. While we are walking, First Sergeant Blankenship is blasting me with one of his sizzling verbal tirades. He is one of the best at mental abuse.

"De Luciano, you puke, you squirming little maggot, who gave you permission to crawl out of your mother's womb, soldier? Why were you ever born? Who allowed you into this man's army, tadpole? Did you come here to offend me, De Luciano? Are you about to cry, De Luciano? Should we call Specialist Likens, our mental health counselor, for you? Should we load you into the wimp mobile right now? De Luciano, you are a disgrace to the uniform. You are lower than whale waste."

I get it, First Sergeant Blankenship. Man, you don't like me, but what is this all about? Am I on a hidden camera? This has got to be a joke being played on me, right? Comedy by conspiracy? Comedic tragedy? I am confused for sure.

Major Kaldenberg's voice shakes me back into the moment, "Leave him with me and First Sergeant Blankenship inside my office here. Also please remove his restraints for me so he can relax."

The MP replies, "Yes, Major."

Blankenship slams the door, and plaster dust sprinkles out from all the cracks around the door jam, rattled loose from years of bad manners and unpleasant behavior.

Major Kaldenberg speaks first, "De Luciano, we know you have never dealt drugs in your life. We know for a fact you have never been in the presence of drugs."

Now I am really confused—didn't we start with this line two years ago right here in this office? They have my attention as the major continues to speak.

"Specialist De Luciano, you have a huge opportunity in front of you. I was sent here from Fort Leavenworth to clean up the 56th Engineer Company, and I want you to help me accomplish that mission, soldier. We had you arrested for appearances only today. We need to create disinformation going forward about your military status. Am I being clear with you, Specialist?"

Mildly confused, I stammer, "Yes sir, totally clear on my end."

The major continues, "I want you to turn and face First Sergeant Blankenship for me, please. Do not take anything personally that happens to you over the next two hours in this office. It is for appearances only, De Luciano. Is that understood, soldier?"

With a grave feeling that impending events somewhat dire in nature are about to befall me, I nod my head silently in his direction. Blankenship jumps in with a left knee to my stomach, which curls me into a fetal position. He follows with a solid uppercut to my right cheekbone that sends my head into the unforgiving wall behind me.

Blankenship starts bellowing, "Specialist De Luciano, I am making it my mission to have you chaptered out of the US Army. I will see to it that you are a disgrace to your community. I will see to it that you never can reenlist in this man's army ever again without an act of Congress."

Blankenship grabs me by my shirt and shoves me into the door. He slams both my neck and head backward with his forearm, securely pinning me to the office door.

Loudly shouting at the top of his lungs, "De Luciano, you are done. You are done. You have been burned. You have been burned, soldier."

Blankenship tiger-tail slaps me three times across my bruised face.

I can feel the salty taste of my blood as it starts overflowing from my split lips. Sweat is starting to bead on my forehead. Violently, I scream out, "Hit me again . . . I didn't feel anything, Sergeant. Hit me again, you can't hurt anybody."

Sergeant Blankenship gladly obliges my request.

He throws me on the muddy floor and starts kicking my rib cage while screaming, "How do you like this, De Luciano? Do you like this, tough guy? Not so tough now, are we? Not so tough now are we, De Luciano?"

His kicks continue while I cover up trying not to laugh. If anyone hears me laughing, we will break our cover. Blankenship is starting to breathe hard after about twenty minutes of his comical beat down, so I put my finger to my lips, "Shoosh."

Major Kaldenberg has been an eager spectator, relaxing and leaning back in his chair while casually cutting his fingernails. Both guys look at each other with quizzical expressions on their faces and then back toward me.

I whisper, "If one of my options is to be released from the army, I put my vote in for that option right now."

Blankenship explodes into another one of his comical tirades, "You sniveling little puke. I should stomp your guts out right here all over this muddy floor. I should rip your head off and pour gasoline down your neck, De Luciano."

In the end, when you get burned, nobody ever admits to anything. Papers get signed, threats are made, IDs are printed and issued, and tracking numbers become assigned.

They offer you a one-way ticket to any major airport in the United States or its territories; then you are sent packing.

If you choose to stay in the city where you are currently stationed, you will receive a pay voucher stamped with a big bold N.P.D, meaning no payment is due.

No Payment Due. N.P.D.

In Closing
A Thought for Us All

The PRC-77 field radio is crackling in my ear. I am armed with an M-60 machine gun, affectionately known as the Pig. I am locked and loaded with a 1,000 round belt of 7.62 mm ammunition. My co-gunner and good friend PFC Popeye is armed with an M-16 rifle configured with an M203 grenade launcher. He is locked and loaded, carrying 300 5.62 mm rounds in reserve. His launcher tube is packed, and he has four 40 mm grenades in reserve for his M203.

We have been ordered to recon the District Utility Plant's powerline trail for the second time in the last three months up in Arctic Valley along an area known as No Man's Land. It is suspected that women are being murdered and buried in No Man's Land.

Popeye and I are being sent down alone again as a fire team. Our last field report was rejected. We have been asked to push down through the area again and to recalibrate our perspective on what we are seeing. Maybe it's an old homestead? Maybe it's a hunting camp? Go figure it out and bring us a dream is how it is stated to us from our immediate chain of command during the briefing.

What is anguish? Distraught, my soul has been torn asunder, as a rag doll tossed upon the heap, discarded by society at the time of my soul's deepest darkness.

Blotches of red cover my face, tears are dripping off my nose, and I am scared, depressed, and suicidal. I can't believe how frightened I am to look back into the mirror.

Why is this agony so clutching? Why is it so deeply seated within my soul?

My head keeps pounding, but the cymbals are gone. The lights have been dimmed low. Exhausted, I need to relieve my pain.

Maybe I can forget if I play my music loud enough while writhing to a broken beat late into a moonless night. All alone and shimmering among the smoke, a candle with its flickering flame guides me, trance-like in my dance.

What's it like to be stood down, forced to listen, and watch while a savage beast kills his victims. Sometimes we were less than five hundred yards away. Law enforcement was not our primary mission—keep your head down, and obey the curfew.

You're hoping it doesn't happen again, please not tonight. Suddenly a gentle flame flickers from far below. *Is that another fire I see down along the tree line?*

Is that a desperate moaning? "Please stop. Please stop."

Is that a frightened woman screaming? "Why are you doing this to me?" "I hate you!"

Why do I hear howling and growling echoing throughout the valley? Is that a dog barking? Have the wolves come home to feed?

Lingering like volcanic ash, ghoulish screams cloud my mind: "Why are you doing this to me? Don't kill me. I have kids. Don't do this to me—no don't!"

The End.

www.ingramcontent.com/pod-product-compliance
Lightning Source LLC
LaVergne TN
LVHW020642100826
845148LV00012B/2303